The IPFW Writing Program Student Handbook

Jennifer Stewart

CENGAGE
Learning™

Australia • Brazil • Japan • Korea • Mexico • Singapore • Spain • United Kingdom • United States

CENGAGE Learning

The IPFW Writing Program Student Handbook

© 2010 Jennifer Stewart

Jennifer Stewart

Executive Editors:
Michele Baird
Maureen Staudt
Michael Stranz

Project Development Manager:
Linda deStefano

Senior Marketing Coordinators:
Sara Mercurio
Lindsay Shapiro

Senior Production / Manufacturing Manager:
Donna M. Brown

PreMedia Services Supervisor:
Rebecca A. Walker

Rights & Permissions Specialist:
Kalina Hintz

Cover Image:
Getty Images*

For product information and technology assistance, contact us at
Cengage Learning Customer & Sales Support, 1-800-354-9706

For permission to use material from this text or product,
submit all requests online at **cengage.com/permissions**
Further permissions questions can be emailed to
permissionrequest@cengage.com

ISBN-13: 978-1-111-46898-9

ISBN-10: 1-111-46898-2

Cengage Learning
5191 Natorp Boulevard
Mason, Ohio 45040
USA

* Unless otherwise noted, all cover images used by Custom Solutions, a part of Cengage Learning, have been supplied courtesy of Getty Images with the exception of the Earthview cover image, which has been supplied by the National Aeronautics and Space Administration (NASA).

Cengage Learning is a leading provider of customized learning solutions with office locations around the globe, including Singapore, the United Kingdom, Australia, Mexico, Brazil, and Japan. Locate your local office at: **international.cengage.com/region**

Cengage Learning products are represented in Canada by Nelson Education, Ltd.

For your lifelong learning solutions, visit **custom.cengage.com**

Visit our corporate website at **cengage.com**

Printed in the United States of America

Introduction

IPFW writing student:

The IPFW Writing Program Student Handbook was created for you to use in conjunction with the text for your writing classes. This handbook addresses everything from English writing course outcomes to IPFW policies and procedures, from IPFW resources to writing tips.

The writing faculty recommend you keep this text for all writing courses, as it will be required in ENG W129, ENG W131, and ENG W233. However, some of the material will be useful not only in many upper level writing courses, but also in other disciplines' courses throughout your academic career.

A handbook should not be read from page one through the end of the text, but instead its sections referenced as you need them. You may need certain sections more than others; for example, you may visit section 5.1 first. Regardless, you should review the Table of Contents to familiarize yourself with the handbook's contents.

This handbook also contains three sample essays from each course (ENG W129, W131, W233). It's important to note that these essays contain both positive and negative elements. All three essays are littered with grammatical errors (that are corrected in the grammar sections of the handbook), so be sure to not use these essays as grammatical models. Their main purpose of the model essays is that they are to be used in class as a discussion tool.

Throughout the text, there are lined, blank pages to allow you to add frequently referenced material or notes to your handbook.

Jennifer Stewart

Acknowledgments

Many IPFW faculty have had a hand in creating *The IPFW Writing Program Student Handbook*.. I would particularly like to acknowledge the following content contributors:

> Tiff Adkins
> Stevens Amidon
> Stuart Blythe
> Betsy Breitenbach
> Cathleen Carosella
> Debrah Huffman

I would also like to thank Lisa Stapleton's Fall 2009 ENG C565/W365 Editing: Theory and Praxis students for their developmental and editing feedback.

This handbook was also produced with the support and guidance of several English Department faculty and administrators:

> Hardin Aasand
> Stuart Blythe
> Stevens Amidon
> The English Department Composition Committee 2008-2010

Table of Contents

1. The Study of Rhetoric

1.1 The Birth of Rhetoric

Rhetoric emerged as a significant field with the birth of the Greek democracy. Democracy creates legislatures and courts where citizens must plead their case, thus the ability to effectively present an argument and persuade members of a group becomes greatly valued.

Traditionally, the first rhetorician is Corax of Sicily in the 5th century B.C. Gorgias of Leontini, Sicilian ambassador to Athens brings rhetoric to the Greeks.

1.2 Defining Rhetoric

Rhetoric can be defined in many ways. The common definition is "an exaggerated or unsupported argument, or use of language."

JOURNAL PROMPT
What differences do you see in these three definitions ? How do you see rhetoric influencing your daily lives?

Aristotle defined rhetoric as, "The art of discovering the means of persuasion for any subject."

A more modern definition is a form of negotiation, which occurs via a text, between various parties in a context.

1.3 Rhetorical Appeals

Aristotle believed there were three methods of persuading an audience

1. Logos: using logic
2. Pathos: using emotion
3. Ethos: using credibility

While we can separate these appeals to study them, most effective writers use all three appeals to move their audiences.

ASSIGNMENT: THE APPEALS
The three appeals are used in all types of writing. Select a piece of non-fiction writing. Identify how the author uses each of the three appeals to influence his/her audience.

1.4 The Rhetorical Triangle

To understand how rhetoric functions, you should understand the rhetorical triangle.

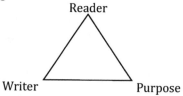

You should consider each part of the rhetorical triangle when composing. One additional element brings Aristotle's formula closer to a modern definition: context.

Context is the *where* of the text, as in where, or under what conditions is the work is written.

4 Categories of Context (from Lauer, *Four Worlds of Writing*)

1. Everyday life
2. School
3. Work
4. Public sphere

As you write, you should ask yourself these questions:

- Why am I writing?

- What context am I writing for?

- Who am I writing for?

- Why do they care?

- What do I want them to do/think/believe?

2. IPFW Course Outcomes

2.1 IPFW Baccalaureate Framework

IPFW faculty have established a framework on which all IPFW students' educations are built. Listed below are the six foundations to a baccalaureate education.

- **Acquisition of Knowledge:** Students will demonstrate breadth of knowledge across disciplines and depth of knowledge in their chosen discipline. In order to do so, students must demonstrate the requisite information-seeking skills and technological competencies.

> **FRAMEWORK CONNECTION ASSIGNMENT**
> Review sections 2.1 and 2.2. Describe how you see the connection between your ENG W129 or W131 class and the IPFW Baccalaureate Framework.

- **Application of Knowledge**: Students will demonstrate the ability to integrate and apply that knowledge, and, in so doing, demonstrate the skills necessary for life-long learning.

- **Personal and Professional Values:** Students will demonstrate the highest levels of personal integrity and professional ethics.

- **A Sense of Community:** Students will demonstrate the knowledge and skills necessary to be productive and responsible citizens and leaders in local, regional, national, and international communities. In so doing, students will demonstrate a commitment to free and open inquiry and mutual respect across multiple cultures and perspectives.

- **Critical Thinking and Problem Solving:** Students will demonstrate facility and adaptability in their approach to problem solving. In so doing, students will demonstrate critical-thinking abilities and familiarity with quantitative and qualitative reasoning.

- **Communication:** Students will demonstrate the written, oral, and multimedia skills necessary to communicate effectively in diverse settings.

2.2 Course Outcomes for ENG W129 and W131

All ENG W129 and W131 courses have the same course outcomes, which are listed below. These outcomes were developed in conjunction with the IPFW Baccalaureate Framework.

- **Rhetorical Knowledge:** Upon completion of the course, students should be able to focus on a purpose; define a thesis; respond to the needs of different audiences; adopt an appropriate stance toward audience and topic; and write in several genres.

> **F.Y.I.** **W129/W131/W233 DIFFERENCES**
>
> While the outcomes for W129 and W131 are identical, generally the methods (the assignments and requirements) an instructor uses to meet those outcomes vary significantly.

- **Critical Thinking, Reading, and Writing:** Upon completion of the course students should be able to use writing and reading for inquiry, learning, and thinking; be able to paraphrase and summarize the work of others; and integrate their own ideas with those of others.

- **Processes:** Upon completion of the courses, students should use multiple drafts to complete an effective text; develop flexible strategies for generating, revising, and editing; engage in a recursive process of writing; demonstrate that they understand the collaborative and social aspects of writing processes; learn to critique their own and others' work; and use various technologies to address a range of audiences.

- **Knowledge of Conventions:** Upon completion of the courses, students should demonstrate that they can recognize and use common formats for different genres of texts; practice appropriate means of documenting their work; and control syntax, grammar, punctuation, and spelling.

2.3 Course Outcomes for ENG W233

Just like ENG W129 and ENG W131, all ENG W233 course have the same course outcomes. ENG W233 course outcomes also reflect the IPFW Baccalaureate Framework.

- **Rhetorical Knowledge:** Upon completion of the course, students should be able to focus on a purpose; define appropriate hypotheses and, eventually, a thesis; respond to the needs of different audiences; adopt an appropriate stance toward audience and topic; demonstrate that they understand how genres shape reading and writing; and write in several genres.

- **Critical Thinking, Reading, and Writing:** Upon completion of the course students should use writing and reading for inquiry, learning, and thinking; be able to define appropriate research questions, pose a hypothesis, and explore that hypothesis through primary and secondary research; demonstrate that they understand the relationships among language, knowledge, and power by synthesizing related sets of texts on a well-defined topic; and integrate their own ideas with those of others.

- **Processes:** Upon completion of the course, students should use multiple drafts to complete a successful text; develop flexible strategies for generating, revising, and editing; engage in a recursive process of writing; demonstrate that they understand the collaborative and social aspects of writing processes; learn to critique their own and others' work; and use various technologies to address a range of audiences.

- **Knowledge of Conventions:** Upon completion of the course, students should follow common formats for different genres of texts; practice appropriate means of documenting their work; and control syntax, grammar, punctuation, and spelling.

F.Y.I.

W129/W131/W233
DIFFERENCES

ENG W233 assumes you have built a foundation for writing in ENG W129 and/or ENG W131. In W233, you are generally given more freedom in topic selection and writing process, as those areas have been covered thoroughly in earlier classes. W233 focuses on developing your writing skills by analyzing your rhetorical choices and your research methods.

Notes

3. University and Classroom Policies

3.1 Student Responsibilities

In most classes, your instructor will have certain expectations of your commitment and dedication to your class. Listed below are some examples of responsibilities you should expect to take on in a writing course.

3.1.1 Your Commitments

- **Time:** Your instructor will expect that you dedicate anywhere from two to five hours of out-of-class work per week. This work could be composing essays, conducting research, or completing assignments. This amount of time is average; you may require more time to be successful in your writing class.

STAYING ON TOP OF YOUR WORK

Take advantage of the free IPFW Student Handbook Planner you receive. Many students become overwhelmed with the amount of homework and assignments they receive throughout the semester. Keeping all work written in one place helps prevent missed assignments.

- **Initiative:** Most instructors will expect you to be committed and dedicated to the class; however, your instructor won't know if you're confused or lost on an assignment or in the class. It's your responsibility to talk to your instructor (see section 3.1.2 for tips on this topic) if you need further guidance or explanation.

- **Respect:** You are expected to show respect to your instructor, your fellow classmates, and yourself. In some classes, you may discuss sensitive or controversial material. Your instructor will expect you to address this material in a mature and reasoned fashion.

- **Dedication:** Your instructors will expect you to keep up with the assignments in the daily portion of the class syllabus. You are expected to arrive to class prepared and on time.

3.1.2 Talking to Your Instructor

Check the syllabus and/or assignment sheets for any information that you should know already. You don't want to ask an instructor, "When are your office hours?" if those times are listed on the syllabus, Blackboard page, or assignment sheet.

If you are discussing an assignment, paper, test, or lecture, make sure that you've reviewed the material and are ready. If you are unclear about points, okay, but that's no excuse for not reading the entire chapter.

When you get to your instructor's office, KNOCK and say "hello" (you'd be amazed at how many students just walk right in and start the conversation). Saying his/her name and, especially if you're in a large class, reminding him/her of yours, is often appreciated.

If you are struggling, explain what you are finding difficult, but don't complain about the class, the material, the lectures, etc. Search for how to improve, not just a quick fix. Sometimes your answer will have nothing to do with the material: improving your study skills, changing your study habits, setting up a study group, using tutoring or supplemental instructions, etc.

Most instructors are more than willing to discuss matters related to, but not necessarily covered in the class – don't be afraid to talk about other areas of the topic or field that you find interesting or want to research.

TIPS FOR TALKING TO YOUR INSTRUCTOR

- If you want to review a paper or have many questions to ask, consider emailing the paper or the questions to your instructor before the meeting. This might help him/her give you more thorough responses.

- If you are absent, ask someone else in the class for notes (ask them before the day, if you know you're going to be absent) and NEVER, NEVER ask an instructor the following: "Did I miss anything?"

Remember that instructors can be just as shy or awkward as you. So don't interpret formality as a dislike of students (or you), but don't be surprised if your instructor is just as friendly as your next door neighbor.

3.2 Instructor Responsibilities

Just as you have responsibilities as a student, your instructor has responsibilities to his/her class. Listed below are some of the responsibilities your instructor should maintain.

- **Availability:** Your instructor should have clear office hours during which you can meet with him or her to discuss questions or concerns you may have about the course.

- **Time:** Your class should not begin before or end after the time posted in the Schedule of Classes.

- **Clarity:** As detailed in the IPFW Writing Faculty Handbook, your instructor should clearly offer the following information:
  - Office location and hours
  - Textbook and supplies
  - Departmental goals for the course
  - Policies on (a) late work, (b) attendance and promptness, (c) plagiarism, (d) formatting of word-processed texts
  - Clear weighting of grades for major components of class
  - A detailed daily class schedule

- **Respect:** Your instructor should foster a respectful learning environment in the classroom.

3.3 Academic Honesty

You are expected to maintain academic honesty in all your courses. Plagiarizing, copying homework, and reusing a paper from one class to another are all forms of academic dishonesty. The IPFW 2009-2010 Undergraduate Bulletin describes plagiarism as "a form of cheating in which the work of someone else is offered as one's own. The language or ideas thus taken from another may range from isolated formulae, sentences, or paragraphs, to entire articles copied from printed sources, speeches, software, or the work of other students." To borrow someone else's writing without acknowledging that use is the worst form of academic dishonesty, which can result in failure for the course as well as sanction from the university. Similarly, the "ghost writing" of a paper can lead to sanction from the University. That is, you should never do someone else's homework for them.

> **F.Y.I. W129/W131/W233 DIFFERENCES**
>
> Often, beginning writing students fear they are plagiarizing. More advanced writing students occasionally cite improperly, and, therefore, plagiarize. If you're unsure whether or not you're plagiarizing, your best bet is to take your draft to you instructor and **ask**. Fixing outright or unintentional plagiarism at the draft stage is the best way to avoid plagiarism penalties.

You must do your own original work in your courses—and to identify that portion of your work which is collaborative with others, or borrowed from others, or which is your own work from other contexts. Whenever you quote passages, borrow graphics, or use ideas from others, you are legally and ethically obliged to acknowledge that use, following appropriate conventions for documenting sources.

You may revise work that you have done or are doing in other courses as long as it meets the following conditions: (1) it is your own work, (2) you plan an extensive revision for this course, and (3) you have informed, and have received the approval of, your instructor. If you have doubts about whether or not you are using your own or others' writing ethically and legally, ask your instructor.

3.3.1 Policy
Academic honesty is expected of all students. You are responsible for knowing how to maintain academic honesty and for abstaining from cheating, the appearance of cheating, and permitting or assisting in another's cheating.

Your instructor is responsible for fostering the intellectual honesty as well as the intellectual development of students, and for applying methods of teaching, examination, and assignments that discourage student dishonesty. If necessary, your instructor will explain clearly any specialized meanings of cheating and plagiarism as they apply to a specific course.

Your instructor will thoroughly investigate signs of academic dishonesty, take appropriate actions, and report such activity properly to prevent repeated offenses and to ensure equity.

3.3.2 Procedures
An instructor who has evidence of cheating will initiate a process to determine guilt or innocence and the penalty, if any, to be imposed.

During an informal conference held within ten (10) class days of discovering the alleged cheating, your instructor will inform you of charges and evidence and allow you to present a defense. Your instructor will make an initial determination after this conference. You may be assigned a grade of Incomplete (I) if the matter cannot be fully resolved before course grades are due in the registrar's office.

3.3.3 Reporting

During the period in which you are permitted to drop courses, the instructor will inform the registrar promptly of any allegation of cheating, so that you cannot withdraw from the course. The instructor who makes an initial finding that academic dishonesty has been practiced will impose an academic sanction. Then, within ten (10) class days, the instructor will supply a written report to you, the chair of your department, the dean or director of your school or division, and the dean of students. The report will summarize the evidence and penalties assessed.

3.3.4 Appeal

If your course grade is affected by the penalty, you have the right to appeal the penalty imposed by an instructor in accordance with the Grade Appeals policy (see section 3.4).

3.4 Grade Appeals

As detailed in the 2009-2010 IPFW Undergraduate Bulletin, if a you wish to appeal your course grade, you must follow the established policy.

> **GRADE APPEAL SUGGESTIONS**
> If you are upset about a grade, WAIT before you go see your instructor. Put the test/paper aside and look at it again later.

The Grade Appeals Policy applies to all students enrolled at IPFW. It can be used by any student who has evidence or believes that evidence exists to show that a course grade was assigned or a similar evaluation was made as a result of **prejudice, caprice, or other improper condition such as mechanical error**.

In appealing, the student must support in writing the allegation that an improper decision has been made and must specify the remedy sought. The student should seek the assistance of the dean of students in pursuing the appeal. During an appeal, the burden of proof is on the student, except in the case of alleged academic dishonesty, where the instructor must support the allegation. The student may have an advisor or friend present during all meetings with faculty members, administrators, and/or committees; he or she may advise the student but may not speak for the student during the meetings.

Grades may be changed only by a university authority upon the decision of the Grade Appeals Subcommittee or by the instructor any time prior to the decision of the Grade Appeals Subcommittee.

3.4.1 Appeal Deadlines

An appeal must be initiated no later than the fourth week of the fall or spring semester immediately following the session in which the grade was assigned. A final decision at each step must be reported within 30 calendar days of the filing of an appeal at that step, provided that this deadline falls within the regular academic year (fall or spring semester). If the deadline falls during the summer, the decision must be reported within 30 calendar days of the start of the fall semester. Each successive step in the appeals procedure must be initiated within three calendar weeks of the completion of the prior step.

Listed below are the steps of the grade appeal process. If appealing a grade, you must follow the appropriate steps.

STEP ONE: COURSE INSTRUCTOR

The student makes an appointment with the instructor to discuss the matter. If the instructor is unavailable, the department chair shall authorize an extension of time or allow the student to proceed to step 2. If the chair is unavailable, the dean of the school shall authorize the extension.

⬇

STEP TWO: DEPARTMENT

If the matter has not been resolved at step 1, the student makes an appointment with the chair of the department, who will direct the student procedurally in making an appeal to the department Grade Appeals Committee (GAC).

⬇

STEP THREE: APPEALS SUBCOMMITTEE

If the matter has not been resolved at step 2, the student makes an appointment with the Dean of the Faculty, who will direct the student procedurally in submitting the case to the campus Grade Appeals Subcommittee.

---

4. Campus Assistance

4.1 Center for Academic Support and Advancement (CASA)

CASA offers a variety of academic support services and is located in KT G23. You can get course-specific, one-on-one tutoring or attend a Student Technology Education Program (STEPS).

CASA's website is located at http://www.ipfw.edu/casa/.

4.1.1 Tutoring

According to the CASA website, the Spot (KT G21) offers you assistance if you have questions about assignments, need formulas or information clarified, or would like to talk to someone about your subject. You will acquire a better understanding of the content, appropriate study skills, and critical thinking skills. These skills will enable you to become more independent, confident learners and critical thinkers--skills that allow efficient and effective learning here at the university and in future careers. You can make an appointment for one-on-one tutoring online via Tutor Trac, or you can stop by KT G21 for a drop-in tutoring session.

4.1.2 STEPS Classes

As indicated on the CASA website, STEPS (**S**tudent **T**echnology **E**ducation **P**rogram**S**) offers free technology workshops to IPFW students. CASA and ITS, working together, offer these workshops to provide you with computer-mediated communication skills needed for college and beyond.

Training sessions are offered in the following areas:

- Microsoft PowerPoint - creating a presentation
- Setting up APA & MLA papers
- The basics of research using the web
- Making the most of IPFW account: e-mail, I drive and myIPFW
- Creating a simple web page design
- Microsoft Word - an introduction to word processing
- Endnote - citing references easily
- A walk through WebCT/Vista

4.2 Helmke Library

Helmke Library has many resources available to IPFW students. Writing students specifically should take advantage of the library's resource librarians and its various course guides.

The library's website is located at: http://www.lib.ipfw.edu

4.2.1 Research Librarians

Sometimes it's difficult to find quality research for your assignment. Other times you find several articles that offer the same information. When this happens, you may want to throw your hands up in the air, give up, and switch assignment topics. Before doing so, consider meeting with a research librarian.

Helmke's research librarians are trained information specialists who can meet with you in person, by IM, by email, or by phone.

In Person—Call 260-481-6505 or visit the Service Desk to schedule an appointment. Walk-in consultations are also available.

By IM—Instant message with a research librarian from the following URL: http://www.lib.ipfw.edu/2896.html. If the chat link reads "ONLINE!" you can speak with a research librarian. You do not have to have a specific IM program to use this function.

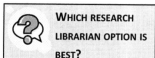

WHICH RESEARCH LIBRARIAN OPTION IS BEST?
Most instructors recommend face-to-face consultations. Then you can work with the librarian at the computer and, potentially, print or save your sources immediately.

By Email—Email your questions to a research librarian by selecting the "Ask a Librarian Email" link on the library's main page.

By Phone—Call 260-481-6505 during library hours to speak to an available research librarian. If all research librarians are unavailable, you can leave a message, and someone will return your call.

4.2.2 Course Guides

For those times when you can't meet with a research librarian, Helmke's librarians have designed course guides for you in a variety of subject areas. These guides were created in consultation with professors and instructors of specific IPFW courses. For example, the ENG W129/W131 course guide details a variety of research needs for writing students such as IUCAT, EBSCOHost, and Internet source evaluation.

> **W129/W131/W233 DIFFERENCES**
>
> *FYI.* While most instructors will introduce various aspects of Helmke's website in all writing courses, it's difficult for you to remember everything that you learn in that day's class. The course guides are excellent reference links when you know you *should know* how to do something, but just can't remember.

Course guides are available for a variety of classes in the following subject areas:

- Anthropology
- Biology
- Business and Economics
- Chemistry
- Civil Engineering Technology
- Communication
- Computer Science
- Consumer and Family Sciences
- Education
- Engineering
- English and Linguistics
- Geography
- Geosciences
- Health
- Physical Education, and Recreation
- History
- Journalism
- Music
- Nursing
- Organizational Leadership and Supervision
- Political Science
- Psychology
- Public and Environmental Affairs
- Sociology
- Women's Studies

Course guides are located on the "Course Guides" link on the main page of Helmke's website.

4.3 Information Technology Services (ITS)

ITS, whose Help Desk is located in KT 206, offers you technological assistance and facilities on campus.

4.3.1 Technological Assistance

The Help Desk has a variety of tools and technicians to help repair disks and troubleshoot computer problems. For assistance, stop by KT 206.

4.3.2 Facilities and Services

Computer labs are located in Kettler Hall, Neff Hall, Helmke Library, Science Building, and Walb Union. Student computer labs are staffed with lab consultants. Generally, the lab consultants can answer various technical questions you may have; however, consultants will not teach a specific program application (e.g. Microsoft Word). For this, you should attend a CASA STEPS program, detailed in section 4.1.2).

ITS also has established several software license agreements for home use of many software programs. These software programs are offered at a greatly reduced price for students. Most purchases can be made at Follett's Bookstore with proof of enrollment—generally a current schedule of classes is required.

4.4 The IPFW Writing Center

The Writing Center, located in KT G19, is open Monday-Friday, as well as Sunday. It offers you free, one-on-one help in writing papers for any class. You may come at any stage of the writing process. Appointments are required; to sign up for a consultation, sign up via Tutor Trac at http://www.ipfw.edu/casa/wc/default.htm. You should bring your syllabus and assignment to your consultation.

> **WHAT KIND OF HANDOUTS DOES THE WRITING CENTER OFFER?**
> The Writing Center offers handouts on academic writing, sources and citation, and grammar and usage. Throughout this text, we will offer some of the most used handouts.

The Writing Center also offers online consulting, free handouts, and workshops on a variety of topics. If you have questions about the Writing Center's services or want to see if there are openings for same day appointments, call 481-5740.

5. Conducting and Citing Research

5.1 Finding a Topic

The following information is reprinted from the Doing Library Research page located on Helmke Library's website.

5.1.1 Choosing your research topic or problem

The first step of a search strategy is to choose a problem to investigate. In some cases you may have been assigned a list of topics from which to choose. If you are responsible for selecting your own research topic, here are some general suggestions:

- Find a topic that interests you and that you can make interesting to your reader.
- Limit yourself to an aspect of the topic that you can adequately research and write in the time allotted. Avoid broad generalities or narrow specialties.
- Choose a topic that can be researched in IPFW's Helmke Library. You must be able to find the information that will support your ideas. By and large, the library does not collect materials that are not directly related to the curriculum.

If you need help with topic ideas, consult CQ Researcher (CQ Press), Opposing Viewpoints Resource Center (Thomson-Gale), or *Editorials on File* (Service Desk D839 .E3). These online and printed resources all cover a wide array of current issues of interest and should stimulate your thinking.

5.1.2 Gaining an overview of your topic or problem

It is easier to narrow your scope to an interesting and manageable paper after you have checked into the background or review of literature on the subject.

One of the best places to get started is an encyclopedia, handbook, or textbook. These tools will provide an overview of your topic and give you hints on ways to limit it. While you are using the encyclopedia, look for an outline at the beginning of the article or the bold-face print and captions within the article. Be sure to note any special terminology, people's names, or events that might be useful in searching for information in other sources.

Most encyclopedias and textbooks also give you a selected bibliography of important books and articles at the end of each major article. This bibliography will almost always list the key sources on the topic and will help identify the authorities on your topic. See especially the bibliographic essays signed by experts at the end of long articles in the Macropaedia section of the New Encyclopaedia Britannica (REF AE5 .E363 1993, shelved in Ready Reference).

In addition to general encyclopedias, the library owns many subject or specialized encyclopedias. To find them, try a **Keyword** search in IUCAT Catalog (Indiana University's online library catalog).

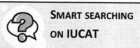

SMART SEARCHING ON IUCAT

Type the search statement: **bioethics and encyclop$** and click the **Keywords Anywhere** button to find the Encyclopedia of Bioethics, for example. By typing encyclop$ with the truncation symbol $, you will find variant spellings, including encyclopedia, encyclopaedia, encyclopedias, etc.

5.1.3 Developing your topic or problem

After you have done some background reading, you should have some thoughts about how the topic can be developed. You may want to:

- Examine a problem or conflict
- Compare and contrast two ideas or individuals
- Consider the causes, effects, trends, or influences on your topic
- Describe a situation, person, corporation, or event
- Persuade your reader

While you determine how to develop your topic, you should also be considering whether your topic is too narrow or too broad to handle. Most people need to restrict their topic to more manageable proportions. Topics can be limited in several ways:

- Time: Concentrate on the 1970s (instead of the 20th century)
- Place: Focus on Iran (instead of the Middle East)
- Discipline: Take an anthropological, psychological, or economic view of your subject
- Specific Event: Examine Woodstock (instead of rock concerts)
- Specific Person (or Group or Work): Focus on Eleanor Roosevelt (instead of First Ladies)

Keep in mind that you can also limit your topic too much, setting unrealistic, "needle-in-the-haystack" search constraints.

5.1.4 Using Subject Pathfinders

If you have an area of interest, but aren't sure where to find information, consider browsing Helmke's section of subject pathfinders, located in the Research Tools portion of the website.

Subject pathfinders can give you a starting point in these topics:

General / Multidisciplinary
- Census 2000
- Current Events
- Reviewing Non-Fiction Books
- Reviewing Non-Fiction Books (PDF)
- Policy Making in Indiana
- West Nile virus

Business
- Accounting
- Banking & Finance
- Business Financial and Operating Ratios
- Company Research
- Core Business Resources
- Economics
- Human Resources
- Industry Research
- Insurance
- International Trade
- Investments
- Labor Studies
- Marketing
- Patents & Trademarks
- Statistical Sources
- Taxation

Education
- Education Law

Health Sciences
- Audiology & Speech Sciences
- Dental Education
- Health Information Technology
- Health Sciences
- Medical Anthropology and Transcultural Health Care
- Nursing
- Evidence-Based Practice in Nursing

Humanities
- Art History
- Literary Criticism: Children's Authors
- Monologue Character Guide (PDF)
- Playwrights and Their Plays
- Theatre

Science/Technology
- Anthropology and Archaeology
- Biology
- Chemistry
- Civil & Architectural Engineering
- Codes & Standards
- Computer Science
- Electrical & Computer Engineering
- Engineering

 WRITING CENTER TIDBIT

If you're having a hard time finding or narrowing your topic, consider visiting the Writing Center to speak to a consultant. Often talking through your topic ideas with another person can help you determine what you want to say in your paper. Writing Center consultants are skilled at brainstorming, thought generators, and idea bouncers. Take advantage of their expertise.

- Engineering, Technology, & Computer Science
- Geosciences
- Mathematics
- Mechanical & Industrial Engineering Technology
- Physics
- Science
- Technical Report Writing

Social/Behavioral Sciences
- Anthropology and Archaeology
- Anthropology Style Guide (PDF)
- Consumer & Family Sciences
- Criminal Justice
- Medical Anthropology and Transcultural Health Care

5.2 Finding Information

When you're asked to do research, you're most likely to head to the Internet. Perhaps you'll do a Google search. Maybe you'll use your AOL browser's search engine. While this research method is effective in determining who that one actor is or how to change the oil in your lawnmower, this method may not be the most effective place to begin your search for academic sources. Whether you have to use substantial and/or scholarly sources, Helmke Library is the best place to begin your source search.

5.2.1 Preliminary, Primary, and Secondary Sources

Preliminary Sources—these are your pre-research sources. As you delve into a topic, you will most likely do a preliminary search through various databases, Internet sites, and IUCAT to ensure that your research topic is viable. As your research topic develops, you may not necessarily *use* all your preliminary sources, as they may no longer support your point.

Primary Sources—this is the research *you conduct*. If you conduct an interview or survey, detail personal experience, perform an observation, execute an experiment, etc., it is your work, and thus, a primary source.

Secondary Sources—this is the research *others have conducted*. When you cite from a book, article, film, study, etc., that is someone else's work, this is considered a secondary source. You have most likely used secondary sources more frequently than primary sources.

5.2.2 Popular, Trade/Professional, and Scholarly Sources

As you progress through your writing courses, your instructors will ask you to use more scholarly sources. The differences between popular, trade/professional, and scholarly are sometimes difficult to determine. Listed below are six areas to examine when determining what type of source you may have.

Article Content

What the author has to say and how the author makes his/her point can help you identify the type of source you've found.

POPULAR	TRADE/PROFESSIONAL	SCHOLARLY
Entertaining and/or informative material of interest to the general public; articles and paragraphs fairly short in length; common language used, assumes no previous knowledge of topic; no bibliography	Articles are fairly short (1-5 pages),; have no abstracts, cite few sources; tend to contain reports of research or news in the field, rather than original studies; and use language familiar to people in the industry or profession	Often original research on a narrowly focused topic; sometimes preceded by an abstract (summary) of the article; terminology used is specialized, assumes some previous knowledge of subject by reader; sources always cited, often in a

Information courtesy "Is Your Journal Scholarly?", Helmke Library

Purpose

Popular, trade/professional, and scholarly sources on a specific topic may have a similar general purpose; however, a close examination into the specific purpose of the article will reveal its true type.

POPULAR	TRADE/PROFESSIONAL	SCHOLARLY
To inform or entertain the general public; produced for profit; sold at newsstands	To communicate trends, developments, product information, concepts and applications useful to those working in the profession or industry	To add to the body of knowledge in a discipline, often by reporting original research or recent experimentation; usually not-for-profit; distributed by subscription only to individuals or institutions (such as your university library!)

Information courtesy "Is Your Journal Scholarly?", Helmke Library

Audience

The audience's knowledge of the topic varies based on the type of source you've selected.

POPULAR	TRADE/PROFESSIONAL	SCHOLARLY
Often not identified, or a staff journalist or reporter for the publication; credentials usually not given	Usually but not always identified; often a professional or specialist working in the particular field of interest	Always identified; professional credentials given; contact information sometimes provided

Information courtesy "Is Your Journal Scholarly?", Helmke Library

Author

Determining an author's origin and credentials can also help establish what type of source you have.

POPULAR	TRADE/PROFESSIONAL	SCHOLARLY
Nonprofessionals, lay persons, general public	Practitioners in a certain business, profession, or industry	Scholars, researchers, or professionals in a particular field of study or discipline

Information courtesy "Is Your Journal Scholarly?", Helmke Library

General Appearance

If you are able to have a copy of the magazine or journal, the appearance of the source itself may give an indicator as to what type of source you have.

POPULAR	TRADE/PROFESSIONAL	SCHOLARLY
Often a slick, glossy, eye-catching cover; color photos; extensive advertising	Often a glossy cover displaying an industrial or professional work environment or product; usually color ads and illustrations	Plain, serious covers; black & white illustrations, charts & graphs; little advertising

Information courtesy "Is Your Journal Scholarly?", Helmke Library

Examples

POPULAR	TRADE/PROFESSIONAL	SCHOLARLY
Consumers Digest; E: The Environmental Magazine; Natural Health; Psychology Today; Rolling Stone; Science News	Advertising Age; American Libraries; Education Digest	Harvard Environmental Law Review; Journal of Consumer Affairs; Journal of Music Theory; Physics Review
	Information courtesy "Is Your Journal Scholarly?", Helmke Library	

Locating Popular, Trade/Professional, and Scholarly Sources

You can find all three types of sources in Helmke's databases and indexes.

POPULAR	TRADE/PROFESSIONAL	SCHOLARLY
Use a database that includes a wide variety of general-interest magazines such as Academic Search Premier (EBSCOhost)	Articles in these publications can be located using an interdisciplinary periodical database like Academic Search Premier (EBSCOhost), or one focused on a trade or profession, such as ABI/Inform Suite for business or ERIC for education	Use a specialized database geared to a particular field, such as PsycINFO (Cambridge Science Abstracts) or Medline (Ovid); databases that include a mix of scholarly, popular, and trade publications may have an option to limit your search to articles in "peer reviewed," "refereed," or "scholarly" journals
	Information courtesy "Is Your Journal Scholarly?", Helmke Library	

5.2.3 Helmke Databases and Indexes

Your instructor will most likely introduce you to some of Helmke's databases and indexes. However, no instructor has enough class time to introduce you to *all* of Helmke's databases and indexes. As you research, you'll need to start investigating different databases and indexes on your own.

When you begin researching, start searching the general and multidisciplinary databases and indexes. They will give you a broader range of articles.

To find any of the databases and indexes listed below, visit **Find Resources By...** on the main page of Helmke's website, and then select **Subject A-Z**.

General & Multidisciplinary

- Academic Search Premier
- Alternative Press Index
- Biography and Genealogy Master Index
- Biography Resource Center
- CQ Researcher
- Dissertations and Theses
- EBSCOhost Databases
- Essay and General Literature Index
- GoogleBooks
- Historical New York Times
- IngentaConnect
- INSPIRE Image Collection
- INSPIRE Indiana Virtual Library
- Lit Finder
- MasterFILE Premier
- McClatchyTribune Collection
- Mental Measurements Yearbook Indexes
- National Newspapers
- Newspaper Source
- OneSearch
- Opposing Viewpoints Resource Center
- Periodicals Archive Online
- Periodicals Index Online
- Readers' Guide to Periodical Literature
- ResearchNow
- Search 360
- TOPICsearch
- Web of Science
- Women's Studies International

Helmke provides you access to information in a variety of specific databases in various areas of study:

- Accounting
- African American Studies
- American History
- American Studies
- Anthropology
- Archaeology
- Architectural Engineering Technology
- Arts & Humanities
- Audiology & Speech Sciences
- Biography
- Biology
- Books
- Business
- Careers & Employment
- Chemistry
- Children's Literature
- Civil Engineering & Civil Engineering Technology
- Communication
- Computer Engineering & Computer Engineering Technology
- Computer Science
- Construction Engineering Technology
- Consumer & Family Sciences
- Consumer Health
- Counseling
- Courts
- Criminal Justice
- Dental Education
- Early Childhood Education

- Economics
- Education
- Electrical Engineering & Electrical Engineering Technology
- Elementary Education
- Engineering, Technology, & Computer Science
- English
- European History
- Finance
- Fine Arts
- Folklore
- French
- General & Multidisciplinary
- Geosciences
- German
- Gerontology
- Government
- Health Sciences & Medicine
- Health Services
- History
- Hospitality & Tourism Management
- Industrial Engineering Technology
- Informatics, Information Systems, & Information Technology
- Interior Design
- Journalism
- Labor Studies
- Latin American History
- Laws
- Linguistics
- Management & Administration
- Maps
- Marketing
- Mathematics
- Mechanical Engineering & Mechanical Engineering Technology
- Media & Public Communication
- Music
- Native American Studies
- News & Current Events
- Nursing
- Organizational Leadership & Supervision
- Peace & Conflict Studies
- Philosophy
- Physics
- Political Science
- Popular Culture
- Psychology
- Public & Environmental Affairs
- Regulations
- Religious Studies
- School Administration
- Sciences & Mathematics
- Secondary Education
- Serials (Journals, Magazines, Periodicals)
- Social Sciences
- Sociology
- Software Engineering
- Spanish
- Statistics & Facts
- Systems Engineering
- Theatre
- Visual Communication & Design
- Women's Studies
- Writing (Creative, Professional, Technical)

Appendix A offers a comprehensive list of databases and indexes organized by the subjects above.

5.2.4 Foraging for Information

When searching for information on your topic, consider the following tips (from Helmke's Information Foraging Worksheet—http://www.lib.ipfw.edu/2049.0.html):

1. Plan your search strategy using the worksheet and SCAN your environment for ideas and resources. Planning and scanning are important steps to becoming an information-literate student and an efficient information forager.

2. Ask yourself
   - What is the nature of your assignment?
   - What keywords describe your topic? Example: standardized tests in high schools
   - What synonyms or related terms describe your topic? Example: tests or testing or assessment, high schools or secondary schools or secondary education

3. Evaluate your results. Most periodical articles and books have subject headings. Are there terms you haven't explored? Example: educational tests and measurement, test bias, achievement tests

4. Use Boolean operators *and, or, not* to develop your search strategy. The shaded areas represent the amount of information found:

AND	OR	NOT
Narrows your search Example: tests and schools	Broadens your search Example: tests or exams	Narrows your search by excluding something Example: tests not eye

Too many results?
- Use more specific terms.
- Use more AND terms.
- Use NOT cautiously.

Too few results?
- Use more general terms.
- Use more OR terms.

5. Use truncation to retrieve variant forms of a term: (test* or assess*) and (school* or educat* or teach*). Common symbols include: * $? # !

6. Use parentheses to group related terms: (tests or testing or assessment) and (high schools or secondary schools) and (research or study)

7. Keep a record of your search history and note the resources that remain to be foraged.

8. Follow the trail of authors and cited references that you discover by reading the relevant literature.

9. Read, digest, and read some more!

5.2.5 Web Sources

When you're asked to do research, you're most likely to head to the Internet. Perhaps you'll do a Google search. Regardless, when you search the Internet, it is important that you are academically critical of the sources you find and cite in your research papers.

5.2.5.1 Finding Credible Web Sources

As you already know, getting hits on a search term when browsing the Internet is not a difficult task, but finding *credible* sources from the Internet can be a bit more daunting.

Helmke's librarians have offered the following tips when searching the Internet:

- Use Google as a starting point. Google's good design and ranked results make it a favorite of librarians everywhere.
- Try a variety of general search engines; while you may find duplicate information, you may also find new sources as well (for a comprehensive list, visit http://www.lib.ipfw.edu/1534.0.html)
- Consider browsing using one of these more specific browsers (all links available at http://www.lib.ipfw.edu/1023.0.html)
  - Blue Web 'n: A Library of Blue Ribbon Learning Sites on the Web—This site takes the searchable directory one step further by subdividing subject categories into Web-based tutorials, activities, projects, lesson plans, hotlists, resources and references. This site is especially valuable for

education students and teachers.

- BoardReader—A search engine of Web-based discussion forums.
- Directory of Electronic Journals, Newsletters and Academic Discussion Lists—A listing of over 7,000 journals, newsletters, zines, and professional e-conferences accessible via the Internet.
- Librarians' Index to the Internet—A searchable, annotated subject directory of around 5,000 Internet resources selected and evaluated by librarians for their usefulness to users of public libraries.

5.2.5.2 Evaluating Web sources

According to Helmke library, because the World Wide Web is a massive, tangled directory of knowledge producers, research, facts, and entertaining tidbits of information, you must be critical about the material you find there. There are many useful guides and tutorials (available at http://www.lib.ipfw.edu/1024.0.html) to help you understand how to navigate and evaluate Web sites.

Is Your Web Site Credible?—from Helmke Library

These criteria were derived from Teaching Undergrads Web Evaluation: A Guide for Library Instruction by Jim Kapoun (1998). There are many additional useful Internet guides and tutorials to help you understand how to navigate and evaluate Web sites. Be sure to apply strict criteria before judging any resource worth your investment of time and attention.

 WEB EVALUATION TIP
Quality and validity are not assured when anyone can publish anything, anytime, without the benefit of scholarly peer review.

Ask yourself if the resource is:

Accurate?
- Does the author provide his or her name?
- Is the information presented verifiable?
- Is the author affiliated with an identifiable group? (e.g., company, university, or government agency)

Authoritative?
- Who maintains the Web site?
- What type of credentials does the author have?
- What is the domain name of the Web site? (e.g. These extensions are often more authoritative: .edu, .gov, or .org)

Objective?
- Is there a stated goal or purpose for the Web site?
- Does the information provide more than one viewpoint?
- Is there a particular bias shown by the author?

Current?
- When was the Web site produced?
- How often is the information being updated?
- How many broken links does the Web site have?

Comprehensive?
- How far back in time does the Web site cover your topic?
- Are there gaps in the information?
- Does the Web site contain important references?

If the website you've selected fails one or two questions, consider verifying the information in a more credible, print source. If it fails several questions, consider the validity of the source altogether.

5.3 Citing Database Information

While there are Internet sites that offer citation page generators and programs such as EndNote, you should be cautious when attempting to use them. Often, they do not create perfect citation pages. Your best bet is to create your Works Cited or References page on your own.

MLA Citation
In-text Citation

If you're citing information from a database in text—regardless of whether you're quoting, summarizing or paraphrasing—you should follow the general in-text citation format of your handbook.

- If you're using a .pdf full-text article, you can use the exact page number the information appears on.

(Johnson 7)

or

if you've used the author's name in a signal phrase (7)

- If you're using an html full-text article, you should use the paragraph the information appears on.

(Johnson par. 7)

or

if you've used the author's name in a signal phrase (par. 7)

Works Cited Page

Pattern:

[Author last name], [First name] [Middle initial]. "[Title of

work]." *[Periodical name]* [Volume number].

[Issue number] ([Published Year]): [Page

number starts]-[Ends]. *[Title of database]*.

[Name of subscription service]. [Medium of

publication] [Accessed day] [Month

abbreviation] [Year].

CITING DATABASE SOURCES

You may be inclined to copy your article URL and paste it into your Works Cited page; however, someone wishing to access that source would not be able to find your article, as they may not have an IPFW account to access your database.

Example:

Berger, James D. and Helmut J. Schmidt. "Regulation of Macronuclear

DNA Content in Paramecium Tetraurelia." *The Journal of Cell Biology*

76.1 (1978): 116-126. *JSTOR*. Web. 20 Nov. 2008.

> **MLA STYLE NOTE**
>
> On an MLA Works Cited and in-text, underlining and italics serve the same function. Select one method for your journals, television show titles, film titles, etc. and stick with it throughout your essay.

APA Citation

In-text Citation

If you're citing information from a database in text, you should follow the general in-text citation format of your handbook. Remember, APA offers page numbers in their citations for quoted material only.

Reference Page

Pattern:

[Author last name], [First initial]. [Middle initial]. ([Publication
    year]). [Title of article]. *[Title of journal]*, *[Volume number]*
    ([Issue number]), [Page number starts]-[ends]. Retrieved
    [Month] [Day], [Year], from [Name of database] database.

Example:

Silva, L. (2007). Epistemological and theoretical challenges for studying
    power and politics in information systems. *Information Systems
    Journal, 17*(2), 165-183. Retrieved February 26, 2007, from
    Business Source Premier database.

Notes

6. Revision and Editing

If you're stuck on a draft and aren't certain what to change, try some of these revision techniques to help you find places in your draft that could benefit from revision.

6.1 The Difference Between Revising and Editing

All of the techniques for revising deal, in some way, with your draft as a whole. When you revise, you're looking at elements that affect the entire draft's organization, length, focus, or clarity.

When you edit, you're looking at individual words or sentences. Sometimes, it can be difficult to tell the difference, but as a general rule, if you're looking at any of the following, you're editing, not revising:

- Typos
- Spelling
- Punctuation
- Grammar errors

6.2 Revising

6.2.1 Revising for Organization

Color code your draft

1. Decide how many main points you have
2. Get that number of colored pencils or highlighters
3. Assign each point a color
4. Read through your draft highlighting or underlining each sentence (or part of a sentence) with the color that matches the sentence's point
5. Take a look at the colors, cut the paper apart, and group each color together.

 COMPUTER TIP

You can color-code with a word processor by using the highlight options. Instead of scissors, use copy and paste to group the colors together.

Gloss your draft

Glossing is summarizing each paragraph in a piece of writing in one or two words.

1. Read the first body paragraph and decide what the topic of that paragraph is
2. Write the topic in the margins of the draft next to that paragraph
3. Repeat with all of the remaining body paragraphs
4. Read what you wrote in the margins
5. Rearrange your paragraphs so that the same, similar, or related topics are together

COMPUTER TIP

You can gloss with a word processor by using the comment feature. See section 7.2.2 for a discussion of the comment feature.

Check your transitions

Transitions are like road signs in your draft. They let readers know where your writing's going next, but they also clarify the connections between ideas.

1. Read through your draft and underline all of your transitions
2. Read the first two paragraphs together
3. Does the transition show the reader the connection between the two ideas?
4. If not, what is that connection? (For different types of connections, see the Writing Center's Transitions handout)
5. Find a transition that does show the reader how the ideas in those two paragraphs connect
6. Repeat for the rest of the draft

COMPUTER TIP

You can check transitions with a word processor by using the underline or highlight options.

6.2.2 Revising for Length

Examine your supporting details

Often, drafts end up short because the paper makes sense in the writer's head, but that doesn't always mean that it will be clear to a reader. In order to determine if you have enough support to make your points clear, you have to try to think like your reader.

1. Look at the length of each of your paragraphs
2. Is any paragraph less than ½ page long? (An approximate standard length for paragraphs in academic writing is ¾ page)
3. If so, can you add reasons, examples, description, explanation, or analysis to make your point clearer for your readers?
4. If you're having trouble coming up with reasons, examples, description, explanation, or analysis, see "Return to prewriting" below

COMPUTER TIP

You can examine your supporting details with a word processor by opening a new document and copying and pasting the supporting details of each paragraph into it's own document. Then, separate each sentence so that it starts on it's own line. Consider what information you can add between each sentence.

Return to prewriting

Sometimes drafts are short because of a lack of ideas. If that's the case, going back to prewriting can help you find additional ideas.

1. Put your draft someplace you can't see it
2. Pick your favorite prewriting technique or a new one and use it
3. Compare your prewriting to your draft to see what new ideas you've uncovered
4. Decide where in your draft those ideas can be added
5. If necessary, repeat

COMPUTER TIP

You can return to prewriting with a word processor by opening a new document and using an electronic prewriting technique such as freewriting or blind writing.

Check for wordiness

If your draft is too long, try tightening your writing by getting rid of wordiness.

1. Look at your first sentence
2. Are you using phrases that don't add any meaning such as "I think that," "I believe that," or "I feel that"? (Since it's your paper, it's assumed that statements are your own ideas unless you tell the reader otherwise with citation)
3. If so, cross those phrases out
4. Are you telling your readers something they already know?
5. If so, consider cutting that information (If your readers already know it, what's the point of explaining it to them again?)
6. Are there any words or phrases in the sentence that mean the same thing?
7. If so, are they necessary for the sentence's meaning?
8. If not, consider getting rid of the repetitious word or phrase
9. Repeat with each sentence

COMPUTER TIP
You can check for wordiness with a word processor by separating each sentence so that it starts on it's own line. Then, examine each sentence individually.

Narrow your topic

A draft that is too long or too short might mean that you're trying to tackle too much in one paper.

If your draft is too long:

1. List each of your main points
2. Decide which main points are the strongest or the most important
3. Are there any main points that aren't as strong or important?
4. If so, consider cutting that main point of your draft is too short:

5. Read your thesis

6. Is your topic too big for the size of your paper? (For example, abortion, global warming, or evolution are topics that might reasonably be covered in a book, but not in a paper.)

7. Read each of your main points by itself

8. Could one main point be the topic of your paper?

9. If not, talk to your professor or a Writing Center consultant about narrowing your topic

---

COMPUTER TIP

You can narrow your topic with a word processor by opening as many new documents as you have main points and copying each into its own document. If you decide to cut a point, save it under a different file name. It might be something you can use for a future assignment.

When you try to cover too much in one paper, you can't go into any depth. By making your topic smaller, you actually give yourself more room for depth and detail, both of which add length.

6.2.3 Revising for Focus
Check your thesis statement and topic sentences

1. Underline your thesis statement and each topic sentence

2. Check your first topic sentence to make certain that it clearly connects back to the thesis statement by repeating keywords in the thesis

3. If the topic sentence doesn't clearly connect, can you change the wording of either the topic sentence or the thesis statement so that it does clearly connect?

4. If not, consider rewriting the topic sentence

5. If you rewrite the topic sentence, read the entire paragraph to make certain that the paragraph supports the new topic sentence

6. If it doesn't, rewrite the paragraph so that it does support the new topic sentence

COMPUTER TIP
You can check your thesis statement and topic sentences with a word processor by opening a new document and copying and pasting only the thesis statement and topic sentences into the new document.

Gloss your draft

7. Gloss your draft following steps 1-4 under "Revising for organization"

8. Compare the first paragraph's summary with your thesis statement

9. Does the first paragraph's topic clearly connect back to the thesis statement?

10. If not, can you rewrite the paragraph so that it does clearly connect?

11. If not, consider cutting the paragraph

COMPUTER TIP
You can gloss with a word processor by using the comment feature.

6.2.4 Revising for Clarity

Get rid of second person pronouns

Second person pronouns are the words "you," "your," or "yourself." Although there are some specific circumstances where second person pronouns are appropriate and effective, they are most often used as stand-ins for first person pronouns ("I," "me," "my," or "myself") or refer to people in general. The problem with second person pronouns is that your reader will not be able to tell if you are referring to you (the writer) or to people in general, and that can create confusion.

1. Read through your draft and circle every second person pronoun

2. Starting at the beginning, decide who you are actually referring to with the first "you"

3. Replace "you" with the appropriate word

4. If you are referring to people in general, see if there's a

more specific word you can use (for example, "you" in this handout refers to people in general, but more specifically, it refers to students or writers. So, if I were to replace "you," I'd use "students" or "writers" instead of "people" or "everyone."

COMPUTER TIP
You can check for second person with a word processor's find feature. Open "Find," type in "you," and click "find next." The word processor will automatically take you to the next second person pronoun in your draft. Replace that pronoun and click "find next." Continue until the word process can no longer find "you" in your draft.

Check for passive voice and replace it with active voice

Passive voice can be confusing for readers because it can hide the subject of the sentence.

1. Read your first sentence

2. Identify the sentence's subject and verb (If it helps, underline them)

3. Is the subject performing the action of the verb?

4. If not, who or what is performing the action?

5. Move the person or object to the front of the sentence (For example: "The paper was written by one student" is in passive voice because the subject, the paper, is not doing the action, writing. The same sentence in active voice would read "One student wrote the paper." Here, the subject, one student, is doing the action, writing.)

COMPUTER TIP
You can check for passive voice with a word processor by separating each sentence so that it starts on its own line. Then identify the subject and verb of each sentence (if it helps, use the underline, italicize, or highlight features).

Have someone else read your draft

No matter how closely you go over your own writing, there will most likely be things that are clear to you but not your readers. The best way around this is to have someone else read over your writing. Ask a classmate, a friend, an instructor, or make an appointment at the Writing Center. To get the most out of your readers, ask questions such as the following:

1. Does the organization seem logical? Is there anything that seems out of place?

2. Is there anything that you want to know more about?

3. Is there anything that you already knew or seems repetitive?

4. Is there anything that doesn't make sense to you?

 COMPUTER TIP

You can have someone else read your draft electronically by emailing your draft as an attachment, but make certain you ask before emailing your work.

6.3 Editing

In recent survey research, Dr. Chris Anson of North Carolina State University and Dr. Robert Schwegler of the University of Rhode Island identified ten writing errors which are most likely to confuse or irritate readers.

Some of these errors are grammatical; others are punctuation errors. In learning to identify and correct these ten errors in your own writing, you will be better able to avoid making those mistakes most likely to bother your readers and limit the effectiveness of your writing.

 GOING BEYOND THE TOP 10

For a more detailed discussion of sentences, word choice, and grammar, refer to those sections in this handbook.

1. Sentence Fragment

Proofreading symbol: frag

A sentence must have a subject and a verb and must make a complete thought. The following sentences are fragments because they are missing one of these three criteria.

Faulty sentence:

But I found out about the Writing Center. Which can really help you write better papers.

Corrected sentence:

But I found out about the Writing Center, which can really help you write better papers.

The use of *which* in the second phrase as a subject makes the phrase fragmented. *Which* is never the subject of a statement.

2. Fused Sentence

Proofreading symbol: fs or fused

Two independent clauses (phrases with subject and verbs which can stand alone as a complete sentence) must be connected with a conjunction, separated with a semicolon, or separated as separate sentences with a period. When they are combined without a conjunction or semicolon, they become "fused" and are often labeled as "run-on" sentences.

Faulty sentence:

Her teacher marked off points for each grammar error and she wanted to be sure she was right.

Corrected sentence:

Her teacher marked off points for each grammar error, and she wanted to be sure she was right.

The faulty sentence above is missing a comma with its coordinating conjunction (*and*).

3. Comma Splice

Proofreading symbol: cs

Sometimes writers try to separate the clauses of a fused sentence by using a comma (,). A comma is not considered to be a strong enough punctuation mark to separate two independent clauses.

Faulty sentence:

There seem to be a variety of reasons that students behave in academically dishonest situations, some researchers take the opinion that students don't feel responsible for their actions while others believe that the students do.

Corrected sentence:

There seem to be a variety of reasons that students behave in academically dishonest situations. Some researchers take the opinion that students don't feel responsible for their actions while others believe that the students do.

Connecting two independent sentences with a comma isn't sufficient punctuation. See page 106 for a list of ways to fix a comma splice.

4. Unclear Pronoun Reference

Proofreading symbol: ref or pr ref

A pronoun substitutes for a noun which has been previously introduced—its antecedent. When a pronoun gets too far from its antecedent, or when there is more than one possible antecedent, the reader may become confused.

Faulty sentence:

You can go into the Center and use their computers to work on your papers; but you can't use them for just anything like in a regular lab, it has to just be your papers.

Corrected sentence:

You can go into the Center and use their computers to work on your papers; but you can't use the computers for just anything like in a regular lab, it has to just be your papers.

Here the use of *it, they,* and *them* can cause confusion for the readers between the references to the writer, the Writing Center, and the Writing Center's computers. When in doubt, be specific.

5. Double Negative

Proofreading symbol: dneg or dn

Using two negative terms together confuses the reader. Avoid using more than one negative word such as *no, none, not, never, neither, hardly, scarcely, barely, haven't, or don't* in a sentence.

Faulty sentence:

As students enter the university and attend their first classes, they may hear several terms from their instructors they may haven't never encountered before.

Corrected sentence:

As students enters the university and attends their first classes, they may hear several terms from their instructors they may haven't ever encountered before.

You can select the phrase *haven't ever* or *have never* as alternatives, but *haven't never* is not considered Standard Written English.

6.   Dangling Modifier

Proofreading symbol: dm

Pay attention to modifying words or phrases at the beginning of sentences. If the modifier does not mention the person, idea, or thing being modified, readers will expect you to name it as the subject of the main clause which immediately follows. If you fail to do this, you confuse the reader.

7.   Missing Possessive Apostrophe

Proofreading symbol: apos

Writers frequently forget to put in an apostrophe (') when using a possessive noun.

Faulty sentence:

Academic dishonesty begins quite early in a students academic career.

Corrected sentence:

Academic dishonesty begins quite early in a student's academic career.

Students without an apostrophe indicates multiple students. *Student's* with the apostrophe indicates possession.

8.   Lack of Subject-Verb Agreement

Proofreading symbol: agr or v agr

Verbs have different forms for the 1st, 2nd, and 3rd person, also for singular and plural subjects. For example the present tense of the verb *to be* varies with person and number:

I *am*   you *are*   he *is*   we *are*   you *are*   they *are*.

When writers mix up these forms, they confuse the reader.

Faulty sentence:

As a student enters the university and attends their first classes, they may hear several terms from their instructors they may have never encountered before.

Corrected sentence:

As students enter the university and attend their first classes, they may hear several terms from their instructors they may haven't ever encountered before.

9.   Lack of Pronoun-Antecedent Agreement

Proofreading symbol: agr or p agr

Nouns are singular or plural in number; so are pronouns. When writers fail to correctly match the two, readers may become confused.

Faulty sentence:

As a student enters the university and attends their first classes, they may hear several terms from their instructors they may haven't never encountered before.

Correct sentence option 1:

As students enter the university and attend their first classes, they may hear several terms from their instructors they may have never encountered before.

Correct sentence option 2:

As a student enters the university and attends his or her first classes, he or she may hear several terms from his or her instructors he or she may have never encountered before.

A student is singular and *their* and *they* are plural. To fix the error, change the language so they match. Notice the correct sentence 1 is less wordy, and, therefore, the better option.

10.   Illogical or Inconsistent Shifts

Proofreading symbol: shift

Writers should have a reason when they shift pronouns from one person to another (i.e. from "I" to "he") and when shifting verb tense. When they don't have a reason, readers may become confused.

7. Using Technology

7.1 MLA and APA Format

Many instructors ask that your homework be formatted in MLA or APA style. Your course handbook offers an example of an MLA- and APA-style paper; Figures 7.1 and 7.2 describe the formatting specifics of the two styles.

Figure 7.1 MLA Homework Format

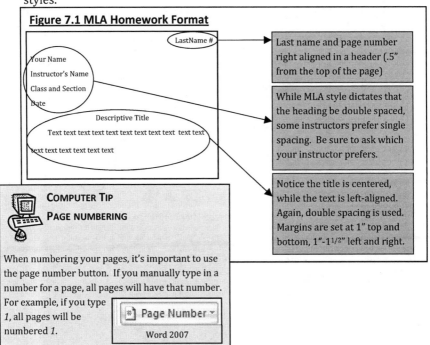

LastName #

Your Name
Instructor's Name
Class and Section
Date

Descriptive Title

Text text text text text text text text text text text
text text text text text text

Last name and page number right aligned in a header (.5" from the top of the page)

While MLA style dictates that the heading be double spaced, some instructors prefer single spacing. Be sure to ask which your instructor prefers.

Notice the title is centered, while the text is left-aligned. Again, double spacing is used. Margins are set at 1" top and bottom, 1"-1½" left and right.

COMPUTER TIP

PAGE NUMBERING

When numbering your pages, it's important to use the page number button. If you manually type in a number for a page, all pages will have that number. For example, if you type *1*, all pages will be numbered *1*.

Page Number

Word 2007

Figure 7.2 APA Homework Format

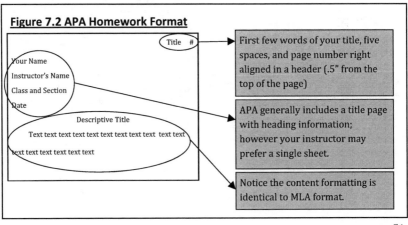

Title   #

Your Name
Instructor's Name
Class and Section
Date

Descriptive Title

Text text text text text text text text text text text
text text text text text text

First few words of your title, five spaces, and page number right aligned in a header (.5" from the top of the page)

APA generally includes a title page with heading information; however your instructor may prefer a single sheet.

Notice the content formatting is identical to MLA format.

7.2 Microsoft Word

ITS supports your use of Microsoft Word; it is also the only word processing program available in computer labs. Because of these facts, many instructors require the use of Microsoft Word **only**. The current version of Word is Word 2007; you may purchase this version at Follett's Bookstore at a reduced student rate. If you do not know how to use Microsoft Word, you can take an ITS STEPS class (see section 4.1.2).

If you have a later version of Word at home, you can visit http://www.microsoft.com to download the Microsoft Office Compatibility Pack for Word, Excel, and PowerPoint 2007 file formats. According to Microsoft's website, by installing

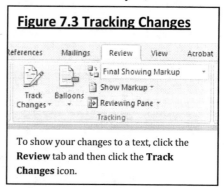

COMPUTER TIP
SAVING YOUR DOCUMENT

If you don't use Word 2007 at home, you can save your document so it is compatible with Word 2007. Be sure to select the *Word 2007* or *Rich Text Format* option when saving.

Save As Dialogue Box

the Compatibility Pack in addition to Microsoft Office 2000, Office XP, or Office 2003, you will be able to open, edit, and save files using the file formats new to Word, Excel, and PowerPoint 2007.

7.2.1 Track Changes

Track changes is a feature in Microsoft Word that allows you, in addition to others, to see your revision process. If your instructor requires that you provide evidence of revision but you don't print a copy of your draft each time you revise, you can use track changes to show your revision process.

If you want others to see the changes you've made to a text,

Figure 7.3 Tracking Changes

References   Mailings   Review   View   Acrobat

Final Showing Markup
Show Markup ▾
Track Changes ▾   Balloons ▾   Reviewing Pane ▾
Tracking

To show your changes to a text, click the **Review** tab and then click the **Track Changes** icon.

click the **Review** tab at the top of the Word 2007 screen (see Figure 7.3).Then click the **Track Changes** icon. To turn off the track changes function, click the **Track Changes** icon again.

To print a copy without your tracked changes, be sure you've selected **Document** in the **Print what** box (see Figure 7.6).

7.2.2 Comment

The comment function is roughly equivalent to adding a sticky note or bubble query to a printed document. The function allows you to insert your own comments into someone else's file (or even into your own) without substantially rewriting the original text. Likewise, it allows others to find your comments quickly. An inserted comment appears on a writer's screen as highlighted text with a bubble attached in the right margin.

Personalizing Your Comments

Word 2007allows numerous people to respond to the same draft. That means you must ensure that writers can recognize who wrote the comments in their file. Usually, you can do that by adding your name or initials automatically to each comment. To do that

Figure 7.4 Identifying Comments

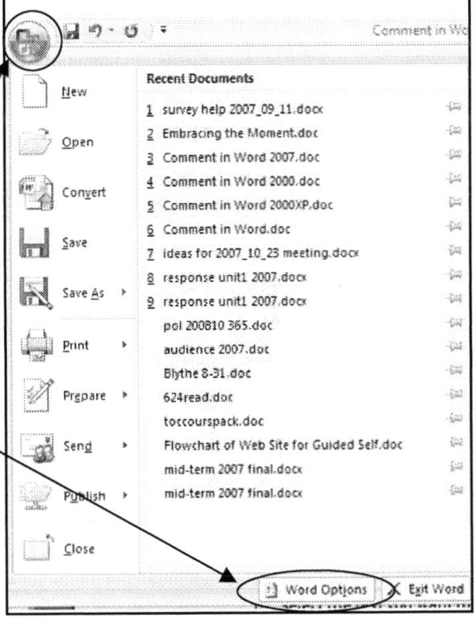

1. Click the Office button in the upper left corner of your Word 2007 screen (an Options window will appear).

2. Click the Word Options button (a "Word Options" window will appear).

3. Enter your name and initials in the appropriate boxes in the "Word Options" window.

4. Click the OK button.

5. After that, your name or initials will appear with each comment you create.

To Add Your Own Comments

Once you have set your identity, you are ready to add comments. To add a comment:

1. Select the text you want to comment on. (You select the text just as you would when copying, cutting, and pasting.)

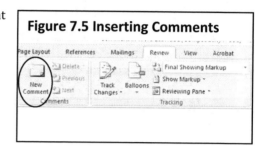

Figure 7.5 Inserting Comments

2. Click the **Review** tab from the top of the Word 2007 screen.

3. Click the **New Comment** icon (see Figure 7.5).

You'll be able to enter text into a bubble in that will appear in the right margin.

To View, Accept, and Delete Comments

You can move from comment to comment by using the **Previous** and **Next** options that appear next to the **New Comment** icon on the **Review** tab (see Figure 7.5). As you move to each comment, you can decide whether to delete it. You can also decide whether to delete all the comments at once.

To Print Comments or Not

To print a set of comments without printing an entire file, begin as you would to print any document:

1. Click the Office button (see Figure 7.4), and then choose **Print** from the column below the button.

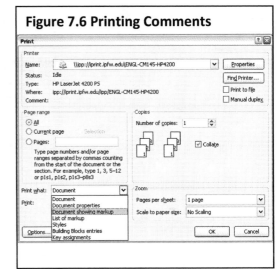

Figure 7.6 Printing Comments

2. Choose **Print** (the Print window will appear).

3. From the Print window, select **Document showing markup** (to see the text plus comments) or **List of markup** to see only the comments (see Figure 7.6) To print the file without the comments, choose **Document** from the Print window (see Figure 7.6).

4. Click the **OK** button.

7.3 Blogging

In order to prepare you for the potential technological components of your career, your instructor may require you maintain a blog. A blog is an online web log. Some instructors may ask you to keep a blog about your research; some may ask you to document your writing process.

Regardless of your blog topic, it is important to remember that blogs are public. Unless you set the parameters of your blog to private, anyone surfing the Internet may stumble across your blog. Thus, you should not treat a blog as a personal journal, but instead as a piece of writing for public consumption. Be cautious of your language and content; several cases have been brought before the courts for defamation. Similarly, if your classmates will be reading your blog, you should remember to maintain a reasoned tone when discussing potentially upsetting issues, as you don't want to unintentionally offend.

To Establish a Blog

One of the most common free blogging sites is Blogger. To set up a blog in Blogger, follow these steps:

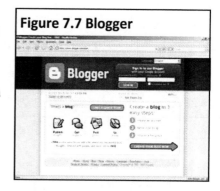

Figure 7.7 Blogger

1. Go to http://www.blogger.com (see Figure 7.7).

2. Select **Create Your Blog Now.**

3. Enter your Google login or follow the steps to create a Google login.

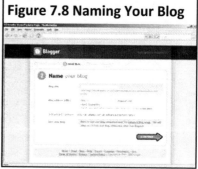

Figure 7.8 Naming Your Blog

4. Select a name for your blog. Remember that this name will become part of the URL for your blog, so try to make it unique. You should select the **Check Availability** link to make sure your blog URL is feasible (see Figure 7.8).

5. Choose a template. This will determine the overall look of your blog regarding color, font, and layout.

6. Begin blogging.

To make changes to your blog, select the **Customize** button. Here you can add or delete posts, make your blog public or private, determine the number of posts viewable, or rearrange your blog layout.

7.4 Creating a Web Page

According to the ITS website, web space is available for individual students to publish noncommercial Web pages related to their university responsibilities.

7.4.1 Setting Up Your Web Space

Your URL will take the form of http://www.students.ipfw.edu/~yourusername/.

Personal Web space, e-mail, and student lab access is provided by your network account. Prior to the start of your first semester at IPFW, you should have activated your computer account at a SOAR session or received instructions in the mail on how to activate your account. This page contained instructions and pointers to on-line help in the use of Web space accounts.

Use of this resource is governed by all IPFW Student Code of Conduct policies, including the IPFW Ethical Guidelines for Computer Users published in the IPFW Student Handbook. Furthermore, you must adhere to the IPFW Web Guidelines for Computer Users (http://www.its.ipfw.edu/policies/webguidelines.shtml). Violation of the codes is subject to disciplinary action.

WHAT ARE THE STUDENT ACCESS LAB LOCATIONS AND HOURS?
Be sure to check the ITS website to see if the lab hours have changed from semester to semester.

Fall/Spring Semester Hours				
Room	M-R	F	Sat	Sun
KT 204A, 217	7a-11p	7a-8p	closed	closed
NF B71	8a-11p	8a-8p	8:30a-5:30p	12:30p-10p
LB 1st Floor	8a-11p	8a-6p	8:30a-5:30p	12p-11p
LB Snack Lounge	24 Hours	24 Hours	24 Hours	24 Hours
SB G15	8a-11p	8a-6p	closed	closed
WU221	8a-2a	8a-2a	8:30a-5:30p	8:30a-5:30p

What Is Provided by IPFW and ITS

- Server space and a Web-based interface, called myIPFW, for logging onto the Web server and uploading, or placing, files there
- Disk space allocation of 10 MB per student or official student organization.
- The Student Technology Education Programs (STEPS) program offers classes in basic Web authoring.

- Various software in the Student-Access Computing Labs for creation of HTML or image files:

    - Microsoft Word can save a document as a Web page

    - HomeSite is an HTML editor

    - Netscape Composer and Dreamweaver are programs that create Web pages without knowing HTML

    - Paint Shop Pro and PhotoShop are graphics programs

- Help using your student lab I: drive and myIPFW via the student lab consultants. (Don't expect them to do your work for you.)

- Student Web Space How To's available at http://www.its.ipfw.edu/training/howto/web/default.shtml.

- Getting Started using Dreamweaver to create Web pages and to upload/download files in your Web space.

What Is Not Provided, or, What You Have to Do

- Backup services for Web files—you are responsible for maintaining current copies of all your Web files on disk

- Training on Dreamweaver, HomeSite, or Netscape Composer—you must learn these programs on your own (but check the help section of both programs; there are great introductions and pointers there)

- Help with converting file formats to HTML, or help uploading files in general--you have to teach yourself if you don't know or understand these concepts

How to Access Your Web Space

If you are using a student-access lab Windows computer you will have an I: drive containing your Web space in the form of a folder named for your username. Files can be copied, deleted, edited, etc. as you would in any other folder. You can also use myIPFW to manage your files.

How to Write Web Pages

On the IPFW campus, there are numerous methods for constructing a Web page.

- Dreamweaver is a special software available on the IPFW network used to create a Web page.

- Netscape Composer can also be used, although the technology may not be quite as good as Dreamweaver.

- If you already understand HTML code, then you might want to use HomeSite.

No matter how you create your Web pages, you need to understand where to save your pages and how to access your Web directory from on campus or from off campus via a browser. Web Page Resources at IPFW offers a lot of basic help.

The STEPS program (see section 4.1.2) offers classes in basic Web authoring.

7.4.2 Web Page Design

A web page is like any other type of writing: it has a purpose and audience. Before you begin developing your website, you should consider these points:

- What is your purpose? Are you creating a site to detail your research about breast cancer? If so, then posting pictures of your dogs or kids may not be appropriate.

- What content will you include? Make a list of the content your website needs or should have.

- How will you organize your information? Decide an organizational structure for your website. Consider using a site tree (see Figure 7.9). In this example, the student has one main page with three links: symptoms, treatment, and risk factors. Then each sub page has its own content.

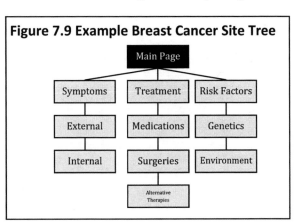

Figure 7.9 Example Breast Cancer Site Tree

Depending on the length of the content, there could be sub-sub pages. Mapping out a site tree can help ensure your web page has a logical organizational pattern.

- What colors and fonts do you want to use? There are many color combinations you can use when creating a color scheme for your web page. Consider visiting http://www.wellstyled.com/tools/ colorscheme2/index-en.html to find a color scheme that works for you. When selecting a font for your web page, pick a font that's clean and simple. *Script*, **balloon**, and trendy fonts can be difficult to read or unprofessional. As always, consider your audience and purpose. A trendy font may be appropriate in some genres and not others.

8. Useful Websites

Many Internet sites exist that can help you in your writing endeavors. As you discover what your own writing or grammatical concerns are, you'll want to conduct topic-specific searches using a reputable search engine.

WHAT'S THAT URL?
Because of the changing nature of the Internet, it's possible the URLs listed here may not work. If so, use your Internet browser to search for the site title to find the proper URL.

8.1 Writing Websites

Purdue OWL

Purdue's Online Writing Lab offers a variety of resources to student writers. According to the OWL, they offer resources in the following areas:

- Writing and Teaching Writing

- Research

- Grammar and Mechanics

- Style Guides

- ESL (English as a Second Language)

- Job Search and Professional Writing

http://owl.english.purdue.edu

<u>Elements of Style Online</u>

William Strunk Jr.'s famous writing manual is available online. Many instructors recommend you revise your draft using the rules in *EoS*.

http://www.bartleby.com/141/

<u>Advice on Academic Writing</u>

This website, created by the University of Toronto, offers many links that will aid you as you write in the academy.

http://www.writing.utoronto.ca/advice

<u>Why We Write Series</u>

This blog, established during the writer's strike of 2008, is a series of essays by prominent writers of TV and film.

http://whywewriteseries.wordpress.com

8.2 Grammar Websites

<u>Grammar Girl: Quick and Dirty Tips for Better Writing</u>

According to its site, "Grammar Girl provides short, friendly tips to improve your writing. Covering the grammar rules and word choice guidelines that can confound even the best writers, Grammar Girl makes complex grammar questions simple with memory tricks to help you recall and apply those troublesome grammar rules."

http://grammar.quickanddirtytips.com/

<u>HyperGrammar</u>

The University of Ottowa offers a comprehensive site that allows you to browse various grammatical issues. The site includes both instruction and review exercises.

http://www.uottawa.ca/academic/arts/writcent/hypergrammar/
grammar.html

9. Professional Writing

9.1 Memos and Emails

Memos and emails are very similar stylistically and are considered the most common form of communication in professional writing. Because of its efficiency and ease, email communication is replacing the printed memo for quick, informal correspondence in the modern work place.

WHAT IS PROFESSIONAL WRITING?

There are many ways to define professional writing. Most simply, it can be defined as the writing done in a work-place setting. Memos, emails, business letters, and reports are types of professional writing that are most frequently used in the work place. IPFW offers several courses that you can take to learn more about professional writing. Additionally, you can earn a professional writing minor to increase your marketability as you enter the business world.

9.1.1 Content

Memos and emails are considered direct messages: they are straightforward and indicate their purpose immediately. Like most pieces of writing, memos and emails have three main components:

1. Opening—indicate the main purpose of the communication

2. Body—provide details regarding the purpose of the communication

3. Closing—offer any direction or call to action for the intended reader

Figure 9.1 Illustrated Memo and Email

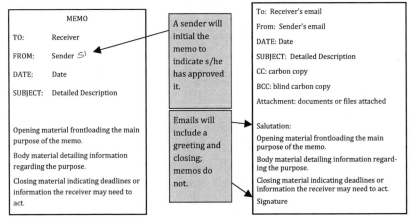

9.1.2 Format

There are only a few formatting differences between email and memo messages as you can see in Figure 9.1 below.

Figure 9.1 offers you an example of block style. Block style is one of the more common formatting choices in professional writing. Generally block style has the following formatting elements:

- Single-spaced text, double spacing between paragraphs
- Generally no indentation for a new paragraph
- One- to one-and-a-half-inch margins
- Twelve-point font

There are variances in block style. If you're unsure what your instructor wants, it's best to ask.

9.1.3 Email Etiquette

Listed below are some basic etiquette suggestions for professional, academic email communication. These have been quoted from Email Replies

(http://www.emailreplies.com).

What are the etiquette rules?

There are many etiquette guides and many different etiquette rules. Some rules will differ according to the nature of your business and the corporate culture. Below we list what we consider as the 32 most important email etiquette rules that apply to nearly all companies:

WHO IS MY EMAIL AUDIENCE?

When sending email to your instructor, consider your tone and writing style. For example, while some instructors may find emoticons humorous, others may find them juvenile. While some instructors may not mind text speak in email correspondence, others may find it inappropriately informal. When in doubt, maintain a clear, respectful, and professional tone.

1. Be concise and to the point
2. Consider your audience and tone
3. Answer all questions, and pre-empt further questions
4. Use proper spelling, grammar, and punctuation
5. Do not attach unnecessary files

6. Use proper structure and layout

7. Do not overuse the high priority option

8. Do not write in CAPITALS

9. Don't leave out the message thread

10. Read the email before you send it

11. Do not overuse Reply to All

12. Take care with abbreviations and emoticons

13. Be careful with formatting

14. Do not forward chain letters

15. Do not request delivery and read receipts

16. Do not copy a message or attachment without permission

17. Do not use email to discuss confidential information

18. Use a meaningful subject

19. Avoid using URGENT and IMPORTANT

20. Avoid long sentences

21. Don't send or forward emails containing libelous, defamatory, offensive, racist, or obscene remarks

22. Don't forward virus hoaxes and chain letters

23. Use cc: field sparingly

9.2 Business Letters

There are many types of business letters. Business letters can give information, sell a product, deny a request, offer a recommendation, or place an order—to name just a few.

9.2.1 Content

While memos and emails are generally written using a direct pattern, some business letters may be written using an indirect pattern. When your audience may have a neutral or positive reaction to your message, you may select a direct pattern. However, if your audience may have an indifferent or negative reaction to your message, you may want to select an indirect pattern.

Direct Pattern	Indirect Pattern
1. Opening—state your main purpose	1. Opening—present buffer to ease into topic
2. Body—provide details	2. Body I—provide reasons for potential bad news
3. Closing—offer direction or action	3. Body II—offer bad news, generally buried within a paragraph
	4. Closing—attempt to reconcile bad news with audience

Notice that both the direct and indirect patterns still have at least three distinct sections: opening, body, and closing.

9.2.2 Format

Figure 9.2 below is an example of a full-block style business letter. A business letter has many formatting elements. Notice there is one blank line between the elements of the business letter. However, to make a letter more presentable, you may include more white space between the return and inside addresses.

Return address—the full address of whomever is sending the letter.

Inside address—the full address of the letter's recipient.

Date—the current date, written out in full.

Salutation—a formal greeting. *Dear* is one of the most common salutations.

Letter text—the text of the letter, which should follow the content suggestions in 9.2.1.

COMPUTER TIP:
TEMPLATES

Most modern word processing programs offer a business letter template, letting you to fill in the appropriate information. However, it is not difficult to compose a clean, simple business letter from a blank document.

Complimentary close—a closing statement. *Sincerely* is a common complimentary close.

Signature block—three to four blank lines to allow for a signature and the typed name and, if applicable, title or position.

Figure 9.2 Illustrated Business Letter

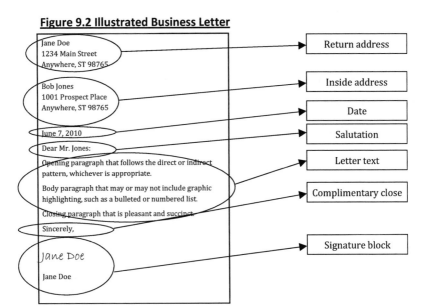

9.3 Employment Communication

Employment communication, your résumé and accompanying cover letter, is arguably the most important written communication you will ever compose. There are many websites, organizations, and services that offer résumé assistance (see section 8). For example, IPFW Career Services, located in Kettler Hall 109, offers drop-in résumé assistance on Wednesdays from 11am-1pm.

WHAT ORDER DO I PUT MY RÉSUMÉ INFORMATION IN?

You want your résumé to have the most important information at the top; therefore, your heading should always be at the top. After the heading, you should include your most important information to least important from top to bottom. For example, if you don't have work experience in your field, but do have a degree in your field, list your education first and work experience last.

9.3.1 Résumés

Many assume the purpose of the résumé is to get you a job; however, the true purpose of a résumé is to get you an interview. The résumé should showcase your skills, education, and experience.

9.3.1.1 Content

You have many options when deciding what to include in your résumé. Ultimately, what you include should be influenced by your audience. Ask yourself the following questions when deciding what to include:

- What does my potential employer need in an employee?
- What job experiences can I highlight that will make me a more appealing applicant?
- Do I have any specific skill sets that I can detail to market myself?

When composing the résumé, do not write in complete sentences; that's what the cover letter is for. All résumés **must** contain the following information:

Heading—your personal information. Include your full name, home address, home/cell phone number(s), and email address. You may also include a URL if you have a **professional** website (MySpace and Facebook need not apply). Also, be sure that your contact email is professional; fuzzybunny23@yahoo.com works fine for friends, but shouldn't be how your employers contact you.

The remainder of your résumé can be selected from the sections below. Depending on your experience, education, skills, and the job you're applying for, your selections will vary.

WHAT ARE ACTIVE RÉSUMÉ VERBS?

You want your résumé to highlight your abilities. So, when listing your employment duties, it's important to use active verbs. Many books and websites offer a list of résumé verbs.
Résumé-help.org: http://www.resume-help.org/resume_action_words.htm
Résumé resource: http://www.resume-resource.com/resumeverbs.html

Objective—what your career goal is. This should be specific. *I want a position that will utilize my skills* is too generic. Who *doesn't* want that? If you're strapped for space on the résumé, you can choose to not include an objective.

Education—your educational information. You should include where you went (or are going) to school, your major and minor, and your GPA. You may also include clubs or activities, honors, and pertinent coursework. Unless you've been in high school in the last few years, only include your college information.

Work Experience—your past employment history. You should include the name of your employer, the city and state of employment, the duration of your employment, your position, and your duties. You do not have to include your employer's full address or the name of your supervisor. When listing your duties, be sure to use active verbs.

Skills and Abilities—any skills you have that you didn't gain from your employment. This section sometimes details any computer skills, typing abilities, or general traits that you wish to highlight to potential employers.

Clubs or Activities—your community involvement. If you don't have any work experience in your field, consider including appropriate volunteer work. For example, if you're applying for a lifeguard position, volunteering at the community pool could be considered appropriate experience.

COMPUTER TIP:
RÉSUMÉS

Most modern word processing programs offer a résumé template, letting you to fill in the appropriate information. However, most business writing instructors recommend you **NOT** use these templates. As your experience grows, it is difficult, and sometimes frustrating, to add to résumé templates. Your best bet is to compose a simple, clean résumé from a blank document.

Interests—any applicable interests you have. The key word in this section is *applicable*. Unless you're applying for a position as a ski instructor, no one really cares if you like to ski.

References—your professional references. If you have space, you may include a list of professional or personal references. Do not use family members as references. Consider employers or professors for professional references. Always be sure to ask permission to use someone as a reference.

9.3.1.2 Format

The visual appeal of a résumé is sometimes just as important as its content. An unappealing or unprofessional résumé may not be read for content at all.

When formatting a résumé, remember to create a professional document by using white space, alignment, tabs, bold, underlining, italics, bullets, and/or numbered lists. Be cautious of overdoing it.

Résumé Tips (for more, see Figure 9.3)

- Be considerate of your readers. Use black ink on white or résumé paper. Try not to use a font smaller than 11 point.

- Be professional. Use a clean font—no script or cartoony bubbles.

- Be consistent with your graphics. If you're going to bold your employers, bold them all.

- Pay attention to white space. Just because you have a lot to include, doesn't mean your résumé should be all text.

- Respect correctness. **Proofread** your résumé. You don't want to lose an interview because you didn't catch a form/from error.

Figure 9.3 Illustrated Résumé

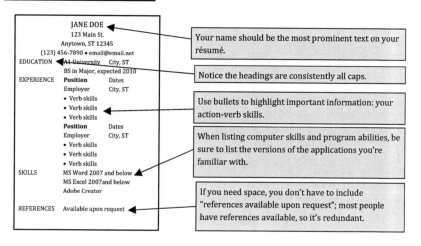

9.3.2 Cover Letters

The purpose of the résumé cover letter is to highlight and elaborate on information contained in the résumé. The cover letter is formatted like any other business letter (see section 9.2.2).

The content of a cover letter should adhere to the following pattern:

Opening—detail how you heard about the position and clearly state your application for the position. If you know someone who works there, this is the place to drop names.

Body I—detail why you're perfect for the position. You should detail information that's introduced on your résumé, **not duplicate it**. Somewhere in this section, you should refer to your résumé.

Body II—detail why you'd like to work *for them*. Visit your potential employer's website and review their mission statement. What about their company appeals to you as a potential employee? **Don't** praise things like vacation time, tuition reimbursement, or hours—that's about *you* not *them*.

WHY DO I NEED A BODY II SECTION?

Some people call this the sucking up section; however, a well developed Body II can show your potential employer that you've done your research and are serious about working for them.

Closing—ask for an interview. Thank the potential employer for taking the time to review your application and résumé. You should indicate that you would like to discuss your qualifications further; this hints that there's more to you than what's on the paper. If you ask them to call you, be sure you have a phone number on the cover letter as well as the résumé; sometime the documents get separated.

Notes

10. Example Student Essays

10.1 ENG W129 Example Essay

The following is an essay for a W129 course. The student was asked to write an evaluation essay that met the following criteria:

- Establishes criteria and states a judgment for each criterion.
- Offers at least three (3) primary sources to support judgments.
- Organizes the material presented in a coherent, logical manner.
- Describes the topic being evaluated.
- Maintains a focus toward the specified audience throughout the essay.
- Uses the conventions of an academic essay and standard written English.

Student 1

Suzy Student

Instructor Smith

ENG W129

October 15, 2009

Writer's Memo

My Rhetorical Situation: I want to persuade IPFW students to go to the Writing Center with their papers. I'm using a persuasive tone and the essay genre.

What I'm comfortable With: I think my information is pretty solid. I got a lot of good information from my interview.

What Areas Need Work and My Plan to Address Them: I think my first draft sounds too rough. I mostly just wrote stuff using my own language, but when I read it, it sounds choppy and repetitive. I'm going to work on combining my sentences and varying my words.

Questions for My Reader

1. I used some stuff from the Writing Center's website. I know we can only use primary stuff, but is that ok?

2. Are my topic sentences too repetitive?

Suzy Student

Instructor Smith

ENG W129

October 15, 2009

The Writing Center

Allot of students have a hard time writing papers.
Sometimes it's because they don't like it. Sometimes it's because
it's hard for them. I have a hard time writing papers myself. But I
found out about the Writing Center. Which can really help you
write better papers. One of the things I like best about the Writing
Center is it's on campus and that makes going there easy. Another
thing I like about the Writing Center is the people who work there
are nice and don't make fun of me if I don't have a lot of my draft
done, they just help me make it stronger. You should go to the
Writing Center, because it has a good location, good consultants, a
lot of availability, and lots of services.

The Writing Center is conveniently located. To find the
Writing Center, you just have to go to the basement of Kettler. It's
in KT G19, right by CASA, down the hall from the common area on
the Subway side. Lots of students hang out there to study, so if you
want to just pop in sometime to have a question answered, that's
really convenient. Also since it's by CASA everything you may need
to get help with your classes is all in one place. They call it "The
Spot." Elizabeth Keller, a consultant at the Writing Center for three
years, says, "I think the location is okay. However, I would much
prefer the Writing Center to be elsewhere (like the library), for
example." She said she wants "More room to spread out

with students, more room to have group consultations, and more room to help with multimedia students. Wherever the location may be, I want it to be HUGE. And with lots of ways for students to express themselves, whatever that may be." Overall, I give the Writing Center's location an A.

Another reason to go to the Writing Center is the consultants. There are many consultants who are available to help you at the Writing Center. I met with Keller to talk about the Writing Center. We talked about my paper for Sociology. Beth and I talked for 30 minutes about my organization, ideas, and how I could make my paper longer. Beth was very kind and helpful. I was kinda afraid she might boss me around but instead she understood the problems I was having and made some really good suggestions. Keller said, "For the last 3 years, I've been a peer consultant. That is, I work with students, one on one, helping them with any part of their writing process (getting started, understanding the assignment, revising what they already have, etc.)." There are about 15 consultants at the Writing Center. They're men, women, young, old, students, and former students. I like that there's a good variety of people who work there. So if you want to get lots of different suggestions, you can meet with lots of different consultants. The consultants get an A.

The availability at the Writing Center is excellent. The Center is open on Sunday through Friday. The hours are: Mon., Tues, Wed, Thu. 10 a.m.-6 p.m.; Fri. 10 a.m.-2 p.m.; and Sun.1-5 p.m. The Center is also open for drop-in consultations if you didn't make an appointment or if you only need a quick question answered.

Theresa Smith, an IPFW freshman, said that she used the drop-in consulting to answer a comma question. Her teacher marked off points for each grammar error and she wanted to be sure she was right. She said, "It was nice to have someone who knows for sure tell me I was right." The Center also offers online consulting. It's available Mon.-Fri. 10 a.m.-6 p.m., but is closed weekends, breaks, and holidays. My English W129 instructor said in class though that it's better to go in person than online. Neither the online consultants nor the Center are available on Saturdays. Because of that, I give the availability an A-.

The Writing Center offers lots of services. Consulting is their biggest service. Keller said, "When I meet with a student, I want to help them do three things: First, I want them to feel comfortable in sharing their writing. I've found that through safe conversation, even the most reluctant or confused student can understand the things that he/she is at the Writing Center for. Secondly, I will do whatever I can as a consultant to show them how to communicate effectively. [I removed stuff here, how do I show my readers that?] it is my hope that the student will see me as an extension of the classroom; we often have copies of their textbooks, etc. that we use during a consultation. And third, I want the student to walk away with something...anything! [I removed stuff here too.] My main goal (especially if this is a student's first visit) is to show the student that writing isn't a mystery; writing is a great way to convey ideas, to convince people of things, and

Student 5

above all to express how they feel." The consultants can help with any writing project—not just stuff for English class.

The Writing center also offers other services. Their website has many handouts that students can use like "Writing a Thesis Statement and Opening Paragraphs," "Annotating a Text," and "Commas." They also offer workshops during the semester. My favorite service (other than the consulting) is the computers that they have in the Writing Center. You can go into the Center and use their computers to work on your papers; but you can't use them for just anything like in a regular lab, it has to just be your papers. So, if you're working on a paper and have a quick question, you can ask the desk consultant. Usually he is available to answer any questions you might have. Because the Writing Center has so many great services, it gets an A.

The Writing Center is a great place to go because of it's location, it's consultants, it's availability, and it's services. According to their Website, "The mission of the IPFW Writing Center is to help writers learn to use language more effectively, produce clear writing appropriate to their purposes and audiences, and develop positive attitudes about writing and about themselves as writers." The Writing Center meets that mission. Every IPFW student who has to write a paper should go the Writing Center for feedback. You won't regret it!

10.2 ENG W131 Example Essay

The following is an essay for a W131 course. The student was asked to write an evaluation essay that met the following criteria:

- Informs the reader about an academic issue.
- Organizes the information in a logical manner.
- Remains a descriptive paper with a moderately neutral tone .
- Maintains a focus toward the audience throughout the essay.
- Uses the conventions of an academic essay and standard written English.
- Uses three (3) or more sources (including two print) and documented appropriately in MLA style.

Student 1

Thomas Student

Instructor Smith

ENG W131

October 15, 2009

Reflective Cover Letter

Instructor Smith and W131 Peers:

I want to inform my audience about the issue of academic honesty. I'm using a neutral, reasoned tone and the academic essay genre.

This is the second draft of my essay. I mostly worked on organizing my points. I've added headings to help my readers follow my organizational pattern. When I took this draft to the Writing Center, the person told me that I may be quoting too much. But I really like all my quotes. Can you help me figure out which I can summarize or paraphrase?

I worked really hard on my Works Cited page. Can you look at it to see if it's right?

For my next draft, I want to try to change some of my quotes to my own words. I also think that I should keep working on my organization. If

---

Thomas Student

Instructor Smith

ENG W131

October 15, 2009

Academic Honesty: Student and Professor Perceptions

As a student enter the university and attend their first classes, they may hear several terms from their instructors they may haven't never encountered before. Academic honesty and it's cousin plagiarism are two terms that students should become familiar with in their college career. According to the IPFW website, "Academic honesty is expected of all students. You are responsible for knowing how to maintain academic honesty and for abstaining from cheating, the appearance of cheating, and permitting or assisting in another's cheating" ("Academic Honesty" par 1). While it's clear students are expected to have academic honesty, what *exactly* it is can be confusing to students. A lot has been said about academic honesty, by both students and professors. This paper will attempt to investigate student and instructor perceptions and definitions of academic honesty.

Defining Academic Honesty

After looking at the IPFW statement on academic honesty it's clear that cheating is considered academic dishonesty, but what else falls under that umbrella? Well, according to Wikipedia, "Academic dishonesty or academic misconduct is any type of cheating that occurs in relation to a formal academic exercise. It can include:

Plagiarism: The adoption or reproduction of ideas or words

or statements of another person without due
acknowledgment.

Fabrication: The falsification of data, information, or
citations in any formal academic exercise.

Deception: Providing false information to an instructor
concerning a formal academic exercise—e.g., giving a
false excuse for missing a deadline or falsely claiming to
have submitted work.

Cheating: Any attempt to give or obtain assistance in a
formal academic exercise (like an examination) without
due acknowledgment.

Sabotage: Acting to prevent others from completing their
work. This includes cutting pages out of library books or
willfully disrupting the experiments of others" (par 1).

So in a writing class academic honesty then can be defined as using
your own thoughts and words or giving credit to the thoughts and
words of others.

But amongst students there seem to be degrees of
academic honesty. Carol Thompson states that, "Clearly, students
are having chances aplenty to see their elders act dishonestly; it
should not be surprising that the students interviewed by Kate
Zernike (2002) for the New York Times asserted that using a
paragraph without attribution did not constitute cheating; echoing
the physicians above, 45% said "falsifying lab or research data" did
not constitute cheating (p. A10)" (2441). Similarly, Elliot Levy and
Carter Rakovski found that students believed the following:
The highest degree of dishonesty was attached to stealing

an exam, submitting another's paper, copying an exam with or without the other student's knowledge, copying a paper or project, allowing someone to submit one's work, using a crib sheet, and allowing another to copy an exam. The lowest level of dishonesty was giving and receiving help on graded material, copying and allowing someone to copy homework, copying from the internet without giving the source, and allowing use of one's paper not knowing that it would be submitted by another student (743). So, it seems that students are not only being given bad examples of academic honesty, but they also consider that honesty is no longer a black and white issue, but many shades of gray.

Most professors, however, still hold to the black and white perspective: there is no "little bit" or "kinda" when it comes to academic honesty. Thompson writes, "The college freshman sitting across from me in my office looked me in the eye and insisted vehemently that he didn't know why his paper was a word-for-word rendition of its twin, which I had found on the Web and was holding next to his own. Another student, having waited 3 days until I returned his graded essay—a cut-and-paste collage of several Web sources labeled "final"—assured me that he had simply given me an incorrect draft. A third brought his mother to the conference; it turned out that not only had she prepared the paper for him, but she also had done the plagiarizing (2439). But professors do seem to struggle with how to address the problem of academic dishonesty in their classrooms. William Badke says, "Education is supposed to be a positive experience. That makes droning on to a room full of students or researchers about the evils of plagiarism essentially anti-educational, as important as the topic may be. It hearkens back to high school when we were shown films of automobile accidents and their victims to scare us into being safe drivers. I suppose we could just view anti-plagiarism instruction as a necessary evil, not particularly educational in the positive sense, but necessary" (59). So instead of becoming the hardnosed lecturer as Badke mentions, Jonathan Malesic thinks that professors should do the following:

> By showing our students what good work is, helping them
> discover what makes it good work, and explaining how we
> can very clearly tell the difference between good and bad
> work, or the relative differences between two authors, we
> are not only improving their minds, but improving their
> "natures." That is a lofty word, one that even humanities
> professors (maybe especially humanities professors)
> hesitate to utter. But maybe we can agree at least that we
> can try to broaden students' perspectives and raise their
> standards, so that they can be better critics -- and better
> self-critics (par 15).

Frequency of Academic Dishonesty

Academic dishonesty begins quite early in a students academic career. Levy reports that, "A survey by the Josephson Institute of Ethics found that 74% of the 12,000 high school students polled had cheated on a test at least once in the past year. The same survey also indicated that students are more likely than in the past to lie to parents and teachers and even to steal (Taylor, 2003). More than 35% of high and middle school students agreed with the statement "I would be willing to cheat on a test if it would help me

get into college" (Gomez, 2001)" (736). Badke also claims that "Cut-and-paste plagiarism from the Internet is increasing, according to the 2005 study from The Center for Academic Integrity (www.academicintegrity.org/cai_research.asp). The research findings showed that 40 percent of almost 50,000 undergraduates questioned have plagiarized from the Net, up from only 10 percent in 1999. What is more, fully 77 percent did not view such activity as a serious issue" (58).

Reasons for Academic Dishonesty

There seem to be a variety of reasons that students behave in academically dishonest situations, some researchers take the opinion that students don't feel responsible for their actions while others believe that the students do. For example, Levy claims that:

Many students who cheat blame faculty for their transgressions, especially professors who fail to respond to what students consider obvious incidents of cheating that occur in their courses (McCabe and Trevino, 2002). Students who perceive that their peers cheat and are not penalized cheat more (Bowers, 1964; McCabe and Trevino, 1993, 1997). Some students complain that their professors are cheating them by spending more time consulting and publishing than teaching or preparing for classes (Fishbein, 1993). ...Notwithstanding outside influences, cheating is strongly dependent on what occurs in the classroom and the biggest factor is the instructor.

Lower levels of cheating have been observed when students believe that cheaters will be caught. And, if students perceive that cheating is likely to be reported, they are also likely to believe that cheaters will be caught and punished (McCabe et al., 2001a, b). (737-738)

Malesic says, "There are probably dozens of reasons why some students plagiarize. They're lazy. They're afraid. They perceive plagiarism to be standard practice. They believe that any means to a good grade are legitimate. What's most astounding, though -- and most insulting -- is that students plagiarize in ways that are so easy to catch. They cut and paste without thinking to cover their tracks. They copy from the most obvious sources possible. They find and replace words and then do not proofread to ensure clarity" (pars. 9 and 10). Badke is more forgiving when he says, "To be charitable, many people have no idea they are committing plagiarism. They use sources carelessly or falsely believe that information can be appropriated at will. One person's plagiarism is another person's research, isn't it? If it's on the Net and it's free to use, why can't I just copy and paste it?" (58).

Some professors take the dishonesty personally; they think the student's cheating is a personal diss. Lang argues, however, "That the last thing on the student's mind, when he made the poor decision to plagiarize, was his personal relationship with you. He did it because he was lazy, or he was rushed for time, or he felt overwhelmed by the assignment. He did not do it to send any message to you about your worth as a teacher, or to test your integrity, or to make your life miserable. He did it for his own reasons and did not expect to be caught, and hence thought little, or not at all, about how his actions would affect you" (par 15). He continues, "When my students violate academic honesty, they are not sinning against me; they are sinning against the standards of an intellectual community they have agreed to join. The proper response is to follow the standards that the community has established for such offenses" (Lang par 18).

Other professors blame our culture for the rise in academic dishonesty. Willen says, "McCabe's comments cited in the *Times* article, though, suggest one way that we might begin to think about it. He explains that "undergraduates say they need to cheat because of the intense competition to get into graduate school, and land the top jobs." The need that students express should not be taken lightly. Surprisingly, McCabe indicates that this need is not an effect of the expectations or requirements for courses being unreasonable; nor are the pressures created by workloads, deadlines and poor time management the primary issues. Instead, this need reflects an anxiety about the future, an anxiety reinforced by their experiencing higher education as professional preparation that is a highly competitive, high stakes endeavor" (56).

Willen also goes on to state, "In this climate what counts most are numbers and results, and those who get results, those who make the grade, regardless of how they go about doing it, reap the benefits. As Callahan suggests, the fact that opportunities for graduates are becoming more limited; that the middle class in American society is shrinking; that the rewards for coming out on

Student 9

top seem astronomical (think for instance of CEO salaries), it is not surprising that, when faced with a choice between preserving one's integrity or doing what is unethical but may ensure some measure of success or security, many students will choose the latter" (56).

Conclusion

Ultimately, it seems that academic honesty and academic dishonesty are two topics that create great debate amongst professors, but there isn't really clear agreement as to its definition or is causes. Malesic points out the irony of academic dishonesty:

> The paradox of plagiarism is that in order to be really good at it, you need precisely the reading and writing skills that ought to render plagiarism unnecessary. If my students could recognize what differentiates their own writing styles from those of authors whose work they find online, then they should also be able to perform with ease all the tasks I require for their essay assignments: to read texts carefully, to determine the relative importance of textual evidence, to formulate a clear thesis, and to defend it convincingly. (par 19)

86

Works Cited

"Academic Dishonesty." Wikipedia. 31 July 2008. <http://
en.wikipedia.org/wiki/Academic_dishonesty>.

"Academic Honesty." IPFW Policies and Regulations. 31 July 2008.
<http://www.ipfw.edu/academics/regulations/
honesty.shtml>

Badke, William. "Give Plagiarism the Weight It Deserves." Online
31.5 (Sep. 2007): 58-60. Academic Search Premier. EBSCO.
Helmke Library, Fort Wayne, IN. 31 July 2008.
<www.lib.ipfw.edu>.

Lang, James M. "It's Not You." Chronicle of Higher Education 54.9
(26 Oct. 2007): 78-78. Academic Search Premier. EBSCO.
Helmke Library, Fort Wayne, IN. 31 July 2008.
<www.lib.ipfw.edu>.

Levy, Elliott S., and Carter C. Rakovski.. "ACADEMIC DISHONESTY:
A Zero Tolerance Professor and Student Registration
Choices." Research in Higher Education 47.6 (Sep. 2006):
735-754. Academic Search Premier. EBSCO. Helmke
Library, Fort Wayne, IN. 31 July 2008 .
<www.lib.ipfw.edu>.

Malesic, Jonathan. "How Dumb Do They Think We Are?." Chronicle
of Higher Education 53.17 (15 Dec. 2006): C2-C3.
Academic Search Premier. EBSCO. Helmke Library, Fort
Wayne, IN. 31 July 2008. <www.lib.ipfw.edu>.

Thompson, Carol C. "Unintended Lessons: Plagiarism and the
University." Teachers College Record 108.12 (Dec. 2006): 2439-
2449. Academic Search Premier. EBSCO. Helmke

Library, Fort Wayne, IN. 31 July 2008.
<www.lib.ipfw.edu>.

Willen, Matthew S. "Reflections on the Cultural Climate of Plagiarism." Liberal Education 90.4 (Fall2004 2004): 55-58. Academic Search Premier. EBSCO. Helmke Library, Fort Wayne, IN. 31 July 2008. <www.lib.ipfw.edu>.

10.3 Example W233 Essay

This essay was written as an argumentative paper for an ENG W233 class. The student was asked to select a debatable issue, present both sides of the argument, and advocate one side. The criteria for the assignment were that the essay should:

- Contain an introduction paragraph which 1) introduces the audience to the issue being addressed, 2) identifies the writer's claim clearly, 3) examines why this information is important to the specified audience, and 4) announces the organization of the paper.
- Offer solid evidence to support the writer's claim (statistics, facts, quotations, surveys).
- Represent and evaluate the opposing points of view fairly.
- Argue reasonably against the opposition and for the writer's claim.
- Maintain a clear focus toward the established audience throughout the paper.
- Appeal to the identified audience in reason, as well as character and emotion.
- Avoid fallacies or errors in reasoning (see Reid 456-458).
- Organize the material presented in a coherent, logical manner.
- Contain a conclusion which 1) restates the writer's thesis, 2) summarizes the support for the writer's claim, 3) echoes the introduction.
- Use signals, cues, transitions, and paragraph hooks to achieve unity between ideas and paragraphs.
- Use conventions of standard written English (appropriate diction, no omitted words, grammar, punctuation, spelling).
- Include evidence of prewriting (freewrites, brainstorming sheets, research documents), drafts, criteria sheets, editing sheets, etc.
- Use seven (7) or more resources and accurately documented works cited, in addition to 10 or more resources on the bibliography page.

Tammy Student

Instructor Smith

ENG W233

October 15, 2009

Dear Readers:

Ok guys, this is my first draft. My purpose is to argue that vaccinations are good for kids. My audience is new parents and/or expecting parents...or really anyone who is interested in this issue.

I'm very happy with my research right now, though I had a hard time finding information to support why parents shouldn't vaccinate their kids. I'm really happy with my visual—I think it adds to the paper nicely.

I'm concerned about my con section. I think it's too short. I also am not sure I cited right—in text or on my bib. I hope to get to the Writing Center to get some help on that one.

Any suggestions you can give me would help,

Tammy

To Vaccinate or Not to Vaccinate: That Is the Question

As new parents prepare for the birth of a child, they are often inundated with information: how to care for their child, what supplies they'll need, the best ways to intellectually stimulate their baby, how to emotionally care for their baby. One of the first decisions that new parents make is regarding vaccinations. Some argue that you should vaccinate your baby following your doctor's advice; others argue that you should be more in control of your child's health. Unless you have a medical degree, however, making this important decision can become confusing and frustrating.

In the last few years, there has been a great debate about vaccinations between the medical community and parents. The resurgence of this debate started when "almost 10 years ago, a researcher in England created a major controversy when he and his colleagues published a report linking the measles-mumps-rubella (MMR) vaccine to the development of autism in children. ("Unexpected effect" par. 1). The desire of parents to prevent the development of autism in their children has caused many to begin to opt out of certain vaccination programs. Many in the medical community believe that this decision is irresponsible; however, it is ultimately the parents who must weigh the pros and cons of vaccinating their baby and make the decision themselves.

The Vaccination Schedule

The American Academy of Pediatrics offers parents and pediatricians guidelines for vaccinations. Figure 1 shows the schedule for 2009.

Figure 1 from the American Pediatric Association

Recommended Immunization Schedule for Persons Aged 0 Through 6 Years—**United States • 2009**
For those who fall behind or start late, see the catch-up schedule

Vaccine ▼ Age ►	Birth	1 month	2 months	4 months	6 months	12 months	15 months	18 months	19–23 months	2–3 years	4–6 years	
Hepatitis B[1]	HepB	HepB		see footnote 1		HepB						
Rotavirus[2]			RV	RV	RV[2]							Range of recommended ages
Diphtheria, Tetanus, Pertussis[3]			DTaP	DTaP	DTaP	see footnote 3	DTaP				DTaP	
Haemophilus influenzae type b[4]			Hib	Hib	Hib[4]	Hib						
Pneumococcal[5]			PCV	PCV	PCV	PCV			PPSV			Certain high risk groups
Inactivated Poliovirus			IPV	IPV		IPV					IPV	
Influenza[6]						Influenza (Yearly)						
Measles, Mumps, Rubella[7]						MMR	see footnote 7			MMR		
Varicella[8]						Varicella	see footnote 8			Varicella		
Hepatitis A[9]						HepA (2 doses)			HepA Series			
Meningococcal[10]										MCV		

In order for parents to make an informed decision about vaccinations, it's important to examine what each vaccination is. The decision to vaccinate or not vaccinate is not an all or nothing decision. Some parents may choose to adhere to part of the schedule or merely adjust their own timelines.

The Argument for Vaccination

The biggest argument for vaccination is that it can prevent your child from getting terrible diseases. Knopper writes:

> The current generation of parents making the decisions about vaccines doesn't remember polio and whooping cough outbreaks. The most vulnerable — newborns and the elderly — are not protected from these diseases. So an older kid could pass it on to a baby sister with disastrous results...."In a highly educated community like Boulder, or, say, the upper West Side of Manhattan, people feel that research is part of their job as parents. But they don't always know how to analyze medical reports, says Chana Goussetis, a Boulder health department

communications specialist."

It makes more sense to have a discussion about parents' opinions about vaccinations with their doctor so they can make an informed decision.

Some argue that vaccinations are harmful to children and that the adverse reactions children get from vaccines do not make them worth the effort. However, in "Immunisation: are parents making informed decisions?" Marfe contends "Overwhelmingly, the majority of immunisations cause no harm hut evidence reveals that there area very few that on rare occasions do so (Johnston 2003). For example, fewer than one child in a million develops encephalitis after MMR vaccine compared with between one in 200 and one in 5,000 who catches measles (NHS 2007)." These odds seem reasonable, but some parents do not want to play an odds game with their child's health.

Physicians are concerned that fewer vaccinations or sporadic vaccinations may lead to the resurgence of illnesses thought to be eradicated in the United States. According to Currie, "A recent measles outbreak in the United States underscores the need to continue immunization programs and raise awareness about the ability of the disease to be imported from other countries. Federal health officials who track measles cases declared the United States virtually free of the disease in 2000, with yearly reported cases between 2000 and 2007 ranging from 29 to 116. But in the first four months of 2008, 64 measles cases were reported in nine states and New York City. Fifty-four of the documented cases were imported from other countries, and 63 of the 64 measles patients had never been vaccinated against the disease." While this example addresses a patient who were imported, who's to say that in the future, we don't have a similar situation. If a child with rubella attends school in a classroom, half of which are vaccinated and half of which are not, is it possible there could be another rubella outbreak?

The Argument Against Vaccination

The phrase "the argument against vaccination" is a bit misleading. Most parents and physicians don't necessarily argue against all vaccination, but instead against either some vaccinations they may deem unnecessary or against the prescribed timetable of the APA. One of their biggest arguments is that children are given too many vaccinations today. According to Jenny McCarthy, "If you look at the vaccine schedule, and you can go on www.generationrescue.com and that's a really good website... the vaccines that you received in 1983 were ten. Today they're thirty-six." Kimmet et al. report that almost 25 percent of parents believe that "children get more immunizations than are good for them."

Some parents argue that having a discussion about vaccinations with their doctors is very difficult. Levi reports, "Though pediatricians and family practice clinicians have a reputation as friendly and approachable, there are reports of parents having their concerns over immunization dismissed and/or disparaged, sometimes aggressively so. One recent study found that 24% to 39% of pediatricians reported they would dismiss a child from their practice if the parents refused 1 of the recommended vaccinations.[50] It is not clear where these children would then go. But when parents' concerns are not effectively addressed, often the end result is that children do not get the medical care they need and deserve. " If a parent cannot have a reasonable discussion with his/her child's medical provider, then how can the parent be expected to make a reasonable decision?

Conclusion

It seems that it is easier to find research to support vaccinating your child than not. Perhaps this is because the medical community more readily disseminates scholarly material that their opponents. While it seems that following the APA's schedule for vaccinations is the way to go, ultimately, it's up to the parents to make decisions for their children.

Bibliography

Abruzzese, Sarah. "Maryland Parents Told to Have Children Immunized." New York Times (18 Nov. 2007): 36. Academic Search Premier. EBSCO. Helmke Library, Fort Wayne, IN. 31 July 2008. <www.lib.ipfw.edu>.

Baker, Jeffrey P. "Mercury, Vaccines, and Autism One Controversy, Three Histories." American Journal of Public Health 98.2 (Feb. 2008): 244-253. Academic Search Premier. EBSCO. Helmke Library, Fort Wayne, IN. 31 July 2008. <www.lib.ipfw.edu>.

Currie, Donya. "Measles outbreak in two states reported." Nation's Health 38.5 (June 2008): 8-8. Academic Search Premier. EBSCO. Helmke Library, Fort Wayne, IN. 31 July 2008. <www.lib.ipfw.edu>.

Diggle, Linda. "Schedule timing and booster vaccinations." Practice Nurse 34.4 (07 Sep. 2007): 9-9. Academic Search Premier. Helmke Library, Fort Wayne, IN. 31 July 2008. <www.lib.ipfw.edu>.

K. L. "Immunization Facts." Working Mother 30.8 (Nov. 2007): 98-98. Academic Search Premier. EBSCO. Helmke Library, Fort Wayne, IN. 31 July 2008 . <www.lib.ipfw.edu>.

Kimmel, Sanford R., et al. "Addressing immunization barriers, benefits, and risks." Journal of Family Practice 56.2 (02 Feb. 2007): S61-S69. Academic Search Premier. EBSCO. Helmke Library, Fort Wayne, IN.31 July 2008. <www.lib.ipfw.edu>.

Knopper, Melissa. "Calling the Shots." E - The Environmental Magazine 18.4 (July 2007): 40-41. Academic Search

Premier. EBSCO. Helmke Library, Fort Wayne, IN. 31 July
2008. <www.lib.ipfw.edu>.

Kotz, Deborah. "Fewer Sticks at Vaccination Time." U.S. News &
World Report 142.7 (26 Feb. 2007): 66-66. Academic
Search Premier. EBSCO. Helmke Library, Fort Wayne, IN.
31 July 2008. <www.lib.ipfw.edu>.

Lett, Dan. "Vaccine--autism link discounted, but effect of "study" is
unknown." CMAJ: Canadian Medical Association Journal
177.8 (09 Oct. 2007): 841-841. Academic Search Premier.
EBSCO. Helmke Library, Fort Wayne, IN. 31 July 2008.
<www.lib.ipfw.edu>.

Levi, Benjamin H. "Addressing Parents' Concerns About Childhood
Immunizations: A Tutorial for Primary Care Providers."
Pediatrics 120.1 (July 2007): 18-26. Academic Search
Premier. EBSCO. Helmke Library, Fort Wayne, IN. 31 July
2008. <www.lib.ipfw.edu>.

Marfé, Eileen. "Immunisation: are parents making informed
decisions?." Paediatric Nursing 19.5 (June 2007): 20-22.
Academic Search Premier. EBSCO. Helmke Library, Fort
Wayne, IN. 31 July 2008. <www.lib.ipfw.edu>.

"No link found between MMR jab and autism." Practice Nurse 35.4
(22 Feb. 2008): 8-8. Academic Search Premier. EBSCO.
Helmke Library, Fort Wayne, IN. 31 July 2008.
<www.lib.ipfw.edu>.

Moore, Alison. "Another injection?." Nursing Standard 22.18 (09
Jan. 2008): 23-23. Academic Search Premier. EBSCO.
Helmke Library, Fort Wayne, IN. 31 July 2008.
<www.lib.ipfw.edu>.

Student 8

"On message, off target." Nature 452.7184 (13 Mar. 2008): 128-
128. Academic Search Premier. EBSCO. Helmke Library,
Fort Wayne, IN. 31 July 2008. <www.lib.ipfw.edu>.

"Preventing illness through immunization." American Nurse 39.3
(May 2007): 5-5. Academic Search Premier. EBSCO.
Helmke Library, Fort Wayne, IN. 31 July 2008.
<www.lib.ipfw.edu>.

"Recommended Immunization Schedules for Persons Aged 0-18
Years -- United States, 2008." MMWR: Morbidity &
Mortality Weekly Report 57.1 (11 Jan. 2008): Q-1-Q-4.
Academic Search Premier. EBSCO. Helmke Library, Fort
Wayne, IN. 31 July 2008. <www.lib.ipfw.edu>.

"Reducing The Pain During Children's Immunizations. (Cover
story)." Child Health Alert 25 (June 2007): 1-1. Academic
Search Premier. EBSCO. Helmke Library, Fort Wayne, IN.
31 July 2008. <www.lib.ipfw.edu>.

Shimabukuro, Tom T., et al. "Potential for Improving Age-
Appropriate Vaccination Coverage by Maximizing the 18-
Month Well-Child Visit." Journal of Public Health
Management & Practice 13.6 (Nov. 2007): 572-577.
Academic Search Premier. EBSCO. Helmke Library, Fort
Wayne, IN. 31 July 2008. <www.lib.ipfw.edu>.

Spencer, Jane. "States Relax Child Vaccine Laws." Wall Street
Journal - Eastern Edition 240.27 (07 Aug. 2002): D1.
Academic Search Premier. EBSCO. Helmke Library, Fort
Wayne, IN. 31 July 2008. <www.lib.ipfw.edu>.

Steinhauer, Jennifer, and Gardiner Harris.. "Rising Public Health
Risk Seen As More Parents Reject Vaccines." New York

<u>Times</u> (21 Mar. 2008): 1. <u>Academic Search Premier</u>. EBSCO.

Helmke Library, Fort Wayne, IN. 31 July 2008.

<www.lib.ipfw.edu>.

Temte, Jonathan L., and Doug Campos-Outcalt.. "ACIP Releases

2008 Child and Adolescent Immunization Schedules."

<u>American Family Physician</u> 77.1 (Jan. 2008): 96-97.

<u>Academic Search Premier</u>. EBSCO. Helmke Library, Fort

Wayne, IN. 31 July 2008. <www.lib.ipfw.edu>.

"An Unexpected Effect Of The Autism-Vaccine Controversy." <u>Child

Health Alert</u> 25 (May 2007): 3-4. <u>Academic Search

Premier</u>. EBSCO. Helmke Library, Fort Wayne, IN. 31 July

2008. <www.lib.ipfw.edu>.

"Updated Pediatric Immunization Guidelines." <u>Nurse Practitioner</u>

33.7 (July 2008): 49-49. <u>Academic Search Premier</u>. EBSCO.

Helmke Library, Fort Wayne, IN. 31 July 2008.

<www.lib.ipfw.edu>.

"Vaccinations: One More Has Been Added...." <u>Child Health Alert</u> 25

(Apr. 2007): 5-5. <u>Academic Search Premier</u>. EBSCO.

Helmke Library, Fort Wayne, IN. 31 July 2008 .

<www.lib.ipfw.edu>.

Webb, Jeremy. "Editorial: Clarity needed over autism and

vaccines." <u>New Scientist</u> 197.2646 (08 Mar. 2008): 5-5.

<u>Academic Search Premier</u>. EBSCO. Helmke Library, Fort

Wayne, IN. 31 July 2008. <www.lib.ipfw.edu>.

Notes

11. Sentences

11.1 Active and Passive Voice

Active sentences are independent clauses with transitive verbs. They follow the basic *subject + predicate* pattern. The difference between active and passive sentences is essentially one of word order. Active sentences follow the pattern of a basic independent clause: *subject + predicate*. That pattern gets reversed in passive sentences.

> The assistant weighed the soil samples.

This simple sentence has a subject (S = "The assistant") for a subject plus a verb (V = "weighed") and a direct object (O = "the soil samples") for the predicate.

If you thought of a sentence in active voice as a kind of equation, it would look like this:

> *Active Voice = S + V + O*

If the sentence were written in passive voice, the order would be reversed:

> The soil samples were weighed by the assistant.

Notice that a number of things must happen to convert an active sentence to a passive form:

1. The direct object ("the soil samples") must be moved to the beginning of the sentence

2. A "to be" verb ("were") must be added before the verb (i.e., "weighed")

3. The subject ("The assistant") must be turned into a prepositional phrase beginning with "by" ("by the assistant")

4. That prepositional phrase must be moved to the end of the sentence (after the verb)

If you thought of a sentence in passive voice as a kind of equation, it would look like this:

> *Passive Voice = O + to be + V + by + S.*

If we were to diagram the transformation to passive voice, it could look like this:

The assistant weighed the soil samples. (Active)

The soil samples were weighed by the assistant. (Passive)

Here are a few other examples:

Parents' desire to prevent the development of autism in their children has caused many to begin to opt out of certain vaccination programs. (Active)

The desire of parents to prevent the development of autism in their children has caused many to begin to opt out of certain vaccination programs. (Passive)

You should understand the difference between active and passive voice for at least three reasons. First, knowing the difference can improve concision (which is the appropriate use of words—not too many and not too few). Notice that sentences in passive voice are more complicated structurally than those in active voice. They're often a bit longer. This is why many composition instructors insist on the active voice; it is simpler and more direct.

Second, knowing the difference can improve paragraph cohesion (which is the sense a reader gets when a paragraph "flows" from one sentence to another). By being able to re-arrange sentences, you're better able to make sure that any given sentence picks up the topic at the end of the preceding sentence. You can also make a conscious effort to begin with a topic that a reader knows, and then work toward new information.

Third, knowing the difference between passive and active voice can help you make conscious decisions about what to emphasize in a sentence. You may have noticed that many in science and technology often prefer the passive voice. This is because they are more interested in what happened, or what was observed, than in who did the observation.

11.2 Parallel Construction

Parallel construction should be used when you're listing or clustering items together. Items in your list should be grammatically parallel because it's stylistically more refined and your audience will better comprehend your points.

Faulty parallelism:

Beth and I talked for 30 minutes about my organization, ideas, and how I could make my paper longer.

noun   noun

phrase

Parallel construction:

Beth and I talked for 30 minutes about my organization, ideas, and paper length.

noun   noun

noun

11.3 Concision

Concision involves saying what you mean in an appropriate number of words. When we talk about being concise, we're not talking about eliminating information. Rather, we're talking about expressing that information in an appropriate number of words. Consider these two sentences:

> Parents' desire to prevent their children's development of autism causes many to begin to opt out of certain vaccinations.

> The desire of parents to prevent the development of autism in their children has caused many to begin to opt out of certain vaccinations programs.

Both sentences announce the same thing, but the first sentence does so in less than half the words. The first sentence is more concise.

11.3.1. Avoid Unnecessary Nominalizations

Writers create nominalizations when they turn verbs into nouns. Consider this list:

Verb	Nominalization
investigate	investigation
appear	appearance
diagnose	diagnosis
record	record
expect	expectation
intervene	intervention
direct	direction
invent	invention

You should learn to spot unnecessary nominalizations because writers often use more words than necessary when they fail to find the best verb for a clause. A good way to avoid this problem is to see whether a sentence could have a stronger verb, which often appears in the sentence already disguised as a nominalization.

> It makes more sense to have a discussion about parents' opinions about vaccinations with their doctor so they can make an informed decision.

> It makes more sense to discuss parents' opinions about vaccinations with their doctor so they can make an informed decision.

Notice that the first sentence contains a nominalization: "discussion." The revision in the section sentence changes the infinitive phrase from "to have a discussion" to "to discuss," which is much more concise.

11.3.2 Use "To Be" Sparingly as a Main Verb

Many writers rely heavily on "to be" verbs (*is, am, are, was, were, be, have been*).

> In the last few years, there has been a great debate about vaccinations between the medical community and parents.

Notice that the writer uses some "to be" verbs in place of stronger verbs, as in "There has been a great debate...between the medical community and parents" vs. "The medical community and parents have debated " or "A debate has raged between the medical community and parents." The writer also relies too often on passive voice, which always requires "to be" verbs.

11.3.3 Rarely Begin Sentences with a Pronoun + "To Be"

Again, too many "to be" verbs can weaken prose. Many sentences begin with constructions such as "This is," "There were," and "It is." Avoid such constructions in most cases (not all cases, but most) because they are less concise than other possibilities. Consider these examples:

> Many in the medical community believe that this decision is irresponsible; however, it is ultimately the parents who must weigh the pros and cons of vaccinating their baby and make the decision themselves.

To revise the sentences above, remember the basic form of an independent clause: *subject + predicate*. Look for the real predicate. In the first sentence, for instance, "must weigh"/"make" could be the predicate (rather than "is").

> Many in the medical community believe that this decision is irresponsible; however, ultimately parents must weigh the pros and cons of vaccinating their baby and make the decision themselves.

11.3.4 Use "Not" Sparingly

In most cases, the meaning of "not" plus another word can be expressed by a single word. Consider these possibilities:

Not phrase	*Concise expression*
not happy	unhappy
do not accept	reject
not successful	unsuccessful
do not care	indifferent
not pleased	displeased
not complete	incomplete

Consider this examples and its revision:

> Some argue that vaccinations are harmful to children and that the adverse reactions children get from vaccines do not make them worth the effort.

> Some argue that vaccinations are harmful to children and that the adverse reactions children get from vaccines negates their value.

This advice about using "not" sparingly is similar to the advice about avoiding nominalizations. To reduce your reliance on both, you have to look for the best verb possible.

11.4 Sentence Variety

While repeating key phrases or terms can create unity in your paragraphs, repeating sentence structure can be, at best, rhythmic or, at worst, monotonous.

For example, in the example W129 paper, the student ends each evaluative paragraph with these sentences:

> Overall, I give the Writing Center's location an A.

> The consultants get an A.

> Because of that, I give the availability an A-.

> Because the Writing Center has many great services, it gets an A.

While the student didn't choose a "the X gets Y" pattern verbatim, it is inherent in each example.

REVISION TIP

You shouldn't worry about sentence variety until after you've written a draft or two of a document. Once you've started revising, consider how you've written your sentences. Do you have many simple sentences? Perhaps you can combine some for a more complex sentence structure. Too many complex sentences? Consider placing your most important ideas in simple sentences; audiences pay more attention to and better comprehend simple sentences.

11.5 Run-on Sentences

Run-on sentences occur when two independent sentences are joined with inappropriate punctuation. There are two types of run-on sentences: fused sentences and comma splices.

> **FIVE WAYS TO FIX RUN-ON SENETNCES**
> 1. Make 2 separate sentences using a period.
> 2. Use a semicolon to make 2 separate sentences.
> 3. Use a comma and a coordinating conjunction to combine the sentences .
> 4. Make one sentence a dependent clause.
> 5. Use a semicolon, transition word (*therefore, however, consequently*), and a comma to separate the 2 sentences.

11.5.1 Fused Sentences

When two independent sentences are combined without punctuation, they create a fused sentence.

Faulty sentence:

Her teacher marked off points for each grammar error and she wanted to be sure she was right.

Corrected sentence:

Her teacher marked off points for each grammar error, and she wanted to be sure she was right.

Connecting these sentence with just a coordinating conjunction (*and*) is insufficient. Adding a comma creates a grammatically correct sentence.

11.5.2 Comma Splices

Comma splices are two independent sentences which are joined by a comma; commas alone aren't strong enough to combine independent sentences.

Faulty sentence:

There seems to be a variety of reasons that students behave in academically dishonest situations, some researchers take the opinion that students don't feel responsible for their actions while others believe that the students do.

Corrected sentence:

There seems to be a variety of reasons that students behave in academically dishonest situations. Some researchers take the opinion that students don't feel responsible for their actions while others believe that the students do.

Just as a coordinating conjunction by itself isn't sufficient to connect two independent sentences, as seen in the previous example, a comma is not strong enough punctuation to connect two independent sentences either. Replacing the comma with a period makes the sentence grammatically correct.

11.6 Fragments

Fragments are groups of words that are punctuated like a sentence but are not grammatically correct. Usually a fragment is missing a subject or a finite verb.

 FIVE WAYS TO FIX FRAGMENTS

1. Connect the fragment to an independent sentence (sometimes with a comma).
2. Connect the fragment to an independent sentence with a double dash (to emphasize).
3. Connect the fragment to an independent sentence with a colon (to indicate clarification or a list).
4. Make the fragment a sentence by adding a subject and/or a finite verb.
5. Remove any word that could be causing the phrase to be fragmented (*because, since, if,* etc.)

Fragment:

But I found out about the Writing Center. Which can really help you write better papers.

Corrected sentence:

But I found out about the Writing Center, which can really help you write better papers.

The use of *which* in the second phrase as a subject makes the phrase fragmented. *Which* is never the subject of a statement.

12. Word Choice

12.1 Formal vs. Informal Language

Generally, you want to use formal language when writing an academic essay. For example, instead of writing:

> That article was totally hard and I didn't understand it at all.

You might write:

> The article was difficult to understand.

The use of textspeak, slang, and contractions is generally considered to be informal language. Some instructors also consider the use of *you* as informal language; it's best to check with your instructor to determine his/her perspective on the use of *you* in each writing assignment.

Depending on your audience, it may be more appropriate to use a mixture of formal and informal language in your essay. Again, this decision is something you should discuss with your instructor.

Listed below are some examples of formal vs. informal language:

Informal	Formal
so	exceedingly
b/c	because
not real clear	unclear
okay	acceptable
awesome	great or impressive
have a ball	enjoy
gazillion	many or innumerable
get it	understand

12.2 General vs. Specific Language

When writing, using specific language is preferable because it helps your audience better understand your point.

THE THESAURUS IS YOUR FRIEND
When revising, many student will use a thesaurus to "spice up" their language. However, be careful that the word you select is an appropriate synonym for your original word.

For example, if you write *says* when introducing a quote, you've wasted an opportunity to clarify for your reader an author's intent. Instead if you write *contends, argues, asserts, criticizes* or any variety of verbs that are more specific than *says*, you immediately let your reader know where an author stands within an argument.

General	Specific
good	exceptional, fantastic
someone	who, specifically, are you referring to here? parents, teachers, students, politicians, etc.
they	
people	
stuff	what, specifically, are you referring to here?
thing	

12.3 Biased Language

Biased language is offensive and shouldn't be used. Your writing can be labeled biased in a few respects: gender, age, and ethnicity.

12.3.1 Gender Bias

Use gender neutral terms when a pronoun is unclear. For example:

A student should watch his language.

In this instance *his* indicates that the student can only be male. To correct the sentence, include the female pronoun as well or make the sentence plural.

A student should watch his or her language.

Students should watch their language.

Similarly, do not use dated, gendered terminology:

Gender biased	Gender neutral
stewardess, steward	flight attendant
postman	postal worker
chairman	chairperson
male nurse	nurse

12.3.2 Age Bias

Be respectful when discussing age in your writing. Instead of describing someone as *old/aged* or *childish,* consider using the term *elderly/mature* or *young.* Often, however, including an indication of age is unnecessary.

12.3.3 Ethnicity Bias

Be conscientious of labeling and stereotyping when describing ethnicity. For example, there are great variances in the terms Chicano, Hispanic, and Latino. When in doubt, research which term you should be using.

12.4 Figurative Language

When writing you can use literal language or figurative language. Literal language is words that mean exactly what they say; this type of language is often preferred in academic writing.

Figurative language is words that exaggerate or imply alternative meaning. Figures of speech and metaphors, for example, are considered figurative language. When you say *Suzanne was crying crocodile tears,* this figure of speech indicates that Suzanne was simulating distress. When you use figurative language, you risk losing your audience's comprehension; therefore, figurative language must be used very carefully.

Notes

13. Grammar

13.1 Parts of Speech

In order to discuss some rules of grammar, it's important that you know the basic parts of speech. The examples of the parts of speech are italicized below.

Noun—a person, place, thing, or idea

It seems that it is easier to find *research* to support *vaccinating* your *child* than not.

Verb—an action or state of being

It *seems* that it *is* easier to find research to support vaccinating your child than not.

Pronoun—takes the place of a noun

So in a writing class, academic honesty then can be defined as using *your* own thoughts and words or giving credit to the thoughts and words of others.

Adjective—describes a noun

So in *a writing* class *academic* honesty then can be defined as using your *own* thoughts and words or giving credit to *the* thoughts and words of others.

Adverb—describes a verb, adjective or other adverb

One of their biggest arguments is that children are given *too* many vaccinations today.

Preposition—shows relationship between two or more words

One *of* their biggest arguments is that children are given too many vaccinations today.

Conjunction—joins words, phrases, and clauses

Ultimately, it seems that academic honesty *and* academic dishonesty are two topics that create great debate amongst professors, *but* there isn't really clear agreement as to its definition *or* its causes.

13.2 Verbs

13.2.1 Subject Verb Agreement

Subjects and verbs should always match.

- Singular subjects have singular verbs.

    Beth is very kind and helpful. (*is* vs. *are*)

- Plural subjects have plural verbs.

    Some professors take the dishonesty personally. (*take* vs. *takes*)

When subjects are joined by *either/or* or *neither/nor* the verb should match the subject that is closest to it.

    Neither the online consultants nor the Center is available on Saturdays.

    Neither the Center nor the online consultants are available on Saturdays.

Because *Center* is singular, *is* is the appropriate verb. However, if the order is rearranged, *consultants* would require *are*, the plural verb.

Indefinite pronouns require singular verbs.

    Some argue that you should...

Subjects and verbs should be located closely together for the sake of clarity. When they are separated, errors can happen.

Faulty sentence:

    There seem to be a variety of reasons that students behave in academically dishonest situations...

Corrected sentence:

    There seems to be a variety of reasons that students behave in academically dishonest situations...

In this case, *a variety* is the singular subject (not *reasons*), thus the verb should be *seems*.

13.2.2 Irregular Verbs

Another common verb error is the incorrect use of an irregular verb. English has many verb tenses; we will focus on the three most commonly used tenses: present, past, and past participle.

PRESENT	PAST	PAST PARTICIPLE
Today I _____.	Yesterday I _____.	I have _____ in the past.

Regular verbs, such as *to walk*, add an *–ed* to the end of the verb to create a past or past participle tense:

PRESENT	PAST	PAST PARTICIPLE
Today I walk.	Yesterday I walked.	I have walked in the past.

Irregular verbs, on the other hand, do not follow such a consistent pattern. Listed below are the most commonly misused irregular verbs (from http://esl-lounge.com). The eleven verbs highlighted, according to the Lancaster-Bergen corpus, account for nearly 50 percent of the irregular use in the US.

VERB	PRESENT	PAST	PAST PARTICIPLE
To become	become	became	become
To begin	begin	began	begun
To break	break	broke	broken
To bring	bring	brought	brought
To buy	buy	bought	bought
To choose	choose	chose	chosen
To come	**come**	**came**	**come**
To draw	draw	drew	drawn
To drive	drive	drove	driven
To fall	fall	fell	fallen
To feel	feel	felt	felt
To find	**find**	**found**	**found**
To get	**get**	**got**	**got/gotten (US)**
To give	**give**	**gave**	**given**
To go	**go**	**went**	**gone**

VERB	PRESENT	PAST	PAST PARTICIPLE
To grow	grow	grew	grown
To hear	hear	heard	heard
To hold	hold	held	held
To keep	keep	kept	kept
To know	**know**	**knew**	**known**
To lead	lead	led	led
To leave	leave	left	left
To lie	lie	lay	lain
To lose	lose	lost	lost
To make	**make**	**made**	**made**
To mean	mean	meant	meant
To meet	meet	met	met
To pay	pay	paid	paid
To rise	rise	rose	risen
To run	run	ran	run
To say	**say**	**said**	**said**
To see	**see**	**saw**	**seen**
To send	send	sent	sent
To set	set	set	set
To show	show	showed	shown / showed
To sit	sit	sat	sat
To speak	speak	spoke	spoken
To spend	spend	spent	spent
To stand	stand	stood	stood
To take	**take**	**took**	**taken**
To tell	tell	told	told
To think	**think**	**thought**	**thought**
To understand	understand	understood	understood
To wear	wear	wore	worn
To write	write	wrote	written

13.3 Pronouns

13.3.1 Pronoun and Antecedent Agreement

The noun that the pronoun refers to is called its antecedent. Pronouns should have a clear antecedent that matches in both gender and number.

Clarity

Often, an antecedent can be vague or unclear. Specifically, watch out for the words *it*, *this*, *that*, *these*, and *those* followed by verbs.

Faulty sentence:

> You can go into the Center and use their computers to work on your papers; but you can't use them for just anything like in a regular lab, it has to just be your papers.

Corrected sentence:

> You can go into the Center and use their computers to work on your papers; but you can't use the computers for just anything like in a regular lab, it has to just be your papers.

Here the use of *it*, *they*, and *them* can cause confusion for the readers between the references to the writer, the Writing Center, and the Writing Center's computers. When in doubt, be specific.

Number

Singular antecedents require singular pronouns, and plural antecedents require plural pronouns.

Faulty sentence:

> As a student enters the university and attends their first classes, they may hear several terms from their instructors they may haven't never encountered before.

Correct sentence option1:

> As students enter the university and attend their first classes, they may hear several terms from their instructors they may have never encountered before.

Correct sentence option 2:

> As a student enters the university and attend his or her first classes, he or she may hear several terms from his or her instructors he or she may have never encountered before.

A student is singular and *their* and *they* are plural. To fix the error, change the language so they match. Notice the correct sentence 1 is less wordy, and, therefore, the better option.

Gender

As to not offend or confuse your readers, pronouns should match their antecedents in gender. Be conscientious of keeping a clear antecedent; particularly potential antecedent referents have the same gender.

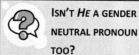

ISN'T *HE* A GENDER NEUTRAL PRONOUN TOO?

Back in the day, *he* was considered an appropriate pronoun to use if the gender was unclear or neutral; however, some readers may find this sexist. Your best bet, if you have a generic or gender neutral antecedent, make it plural: *they* offends no one.

Faulty sentence:

> Theresa Smith, an IPFW freshman, said that she used the drop-in consulting to answer a comma question. Her teacher marked off points for each grammar error and she wanted to be sure she was right.

Correct sentence:

> Theresa Smith, an IPFW freshman, said that she used the drop-in consulting to answer a comma question. Her teacher marked off points for each grammar error and Smith wanted to be sure she was right.

In this example, *she* could refer to either the student or the instructor (as the instructor's gender is not specified). When in doubt, restate the antecedent for the sake of clarity.

13.3.2 Pronoun Case

There are three main cases: objective, subjective, and possessive. Depending on what function the pronoun serves in the sentence you're writing, the case will vary. *This, that, these, those,* and *which* do not change case.

SUBJECT	OBJECT	POSSESSION
I	me	my/mine
you	you	your/yours
he, she, it	him, her, it	his, her/hers, it/its
we	us	our/ours
they	them	their/theirs
who	whom	whose

Most native English speakers can hear when they use the wrong case. *Him is going to the store* shouldn't sound correct. However, there are special instances in which pronoun case can get tricky.

- When *and* is used, you can select the wrong case. To solve this dilemma, remove the *and* phrase from the sentence, and check your pronoun case.

> **ISN'T IT ALWAYS "AND I"?**
> While all our third grade English teachers drilled the "So-and-so **and I**" rule into our noggins, "and I" isn't always correct. "And I" follows the case rule just like any other pronoun. If it's a subject, "and I" is appropriate. If it's an object, "and me" is appropriate.

Faulty sentence:

Send the report to Bob and I.

Correct sentence:

Sent the report to Bob and me.

If you remove *Bob and* from the sentence, the proper pronoun choice is clear. *Send the report to I* uses the incorrect case and sounds awkward.

- When a pronoun follows any form of the verb *to be*, select the subject case.

It is she who should be concerned.

This particular pronoun rule is frequently broken. When in doubt, rearrange your sentence.

- When making comparisons with *than* or *as* be cautious of your case; it can change the meaning of your sentence.

Faulty sentence:

> She believes in capital punishment more than him.

Correct sentence:

> She believes in capital punishment more than he.

To better understand this rule, it's important to finish the thought. The faulty sentence implies that she believes in capital punishment more than she believes in him. The corrected sentence fulfills the author's intent: she believes in capital punishment more than he does.

- *Who* vs. *Whom*: Sometimes the best way to decide whether you should use *who* or *whom* is to replace the *who/whom* with *he/him*. If *he* is appropriate, choose *who*. If *him* is appropriate, choose *whom*.

> She will bring whomever she wants.

In this instance, you would say she will bring *him*, so *whom* becomes the correct choice.

13.3.3 Collective Pronouns

Collective pronouns refer to a large group or organization such as *team*, *committee*, *family*, or *group*.

These antecedents also generally require singular pronouns.

> The Writing Center offers lots of services. Handouts is one of *its* services.

Because *its* refers back to the Center as a whole (because the Center as an entity offers handouts), the singular pronoun is appropriate.

However, there are instances in which a collective antecedent can have a plural pronoun.

> The Writing Center offers lots of services. Consulting with students is *their* biggest service.

Because *their* refers, indirectly, to the Center's staff (as they are the ones who consult with students, not the Center as an entity), *their* is appropriate.

13.3.4 Indefinite Pronouns

Some pronouns aren't clearly singular or plural and, thus, create agreement issues.

Singular

another, anybody, anyone, anything, each, either, everybody, everyone, everything, little, much, neither, nobody, no one, nothing, one, other, somebody, someone, something

> Somebody hit me. (*hit* vs. *hits*)

Plural

both, few, many, others, several

> Many are coming to dinner. (*are* vs. *is*)

Singular or Plural

all, any, more, most, none, some

AGREEMENT TIP

For pronouns that can be singular or plural, look to identifiers within the context of the sentence for agreement clues.

Notes

_____

_____

_____

_____

_____

_____

_____

_____

_____

_____

_____

14. Punctuation

14.1 The Period (.)

**WORD PROCESSING
THE PERIOD**

When using a typewriter, the common rule was two spaces after the period. However, with the word processor taking over the job of the typewriter, the rule is changing. A single space after the period is now considered acceptable as well.

14.1.1 End a statment
Use a period to indicate the end of a sentence.

14.1.2 Polite Request
Use a period to end a polite request. While the sentence may be structured as a question, the writer intends that the audience will comply with his/her request.

Will you send me the forms immediately.

14.2 The Question Mark (?)
Use a question mark to end a query.

How can parents be expected to make such a decision?

If you're tagging a question at the end of a statement, do not forget to separate the question tag with a comma.

They are being unreasonable, right?

The use of multiple question marks to provide emphasis is considered informal and not recommended for academic writing.

14.3 The Exclamation Point (!)
Use an exclamation mark to indicate strong feelings or excitement.

You won't regret it!

Exclamation marks can be considered juvenile or informal by many instructors; use them sparingly, if at all, in academic writing.

14.4 The Comma (,)
14.4.1 Introductory Words or Phrases
Commas are required after introductory words, phrases, or clauses.

Even though I'm tired, I intend to finish my work.

14.4.2 Restrictive and Non-restrictive Clauses

RESTRICTIVE CLAUSES VS. NON-RESTRICTIVE CLAUSES

A restrictive clause contains information that is imperative to the meaning of the sentence. A non-restrictive clause contains information that adds to the sentence but does not affect the true meaning of the sentence.

Use a comma to set off non-restrictive clauses only.

> Theresa Smith, an IPFW freshman, said that she used the drop-in consulting to answer a comma question.

The phrase *an IPFW freshman* is not imperative to the meaning of the sentence, thus, can be set off with commas.

14.4.3 Compound Sentences

Use a comma to separate two independent clauses that are joined by a coordinating conjunction—*for, and, nor, but, or, yet*, and *so*, the acronym FANBOYS can be used as a memory aid (refer to run-on).

> So, it seems that students are not only being given bad examples of academic honesty, but they also consider that honesty is no longer a black and white issue, but many shades of gray.

The two sentences before and after *, but* are independent sentences. The best way to test the sentences quickly is to read them aloud separately. If they make sense, they're most likely independent sentences.

14.4.4 Items in a Series

Use a comma to separate items in a series of three or more.

> They're men, women, young, old, students, and former students.

14.4.5 Other Comma Rules

- Use commas to set off the year if the month and date are included.

> January 20, 1994, is my birthday.

- Use commas to set off the state, county, or country if it follows a city.

COMMA BEFORE THE *AND* IN A LIST

Always include a comma before the and when separating items in a list of three or more. It's a convention of journalistic writing to remove the final comma in a series; however, in your English classes, you should follow Standard Written English which dictates that the final comma be included.

She's traveling to Mobile, AL, next week.

14.4.6 Common Comma Errors

Separating a Subject and its Verb

Unless the comma is being used with a non-restrictive phrase, you should never separate a subject and its verb with a comma.

> You should go to the Writing Center, because it has a good location, good consultants, a lot of availability, and lots of services.

Items in a List

Do not use a comma if your list only contains two items.

Independent Clause Followed by Dependent Clause

If your dependent clause follows your independent clause, the comma is unnecessary.

14.5 The Semicolon (;)

WHY USE A SEMICOLON?
You can show your reader that the ideas in the two sentences you've connected are related. Also, using a semicolon to combine sentences is a good way to create sentence variety in your writing.

14.5.1 Separating Independent Clauses

Use a semicolon to separate two independent clauses.

Faulty sentence:

You can go into the Center and use their computers to work on your papers; but you can't use them for just anything like in a regular lab, it has to just be your papers.

Correct sentence:

You can go into the Center and use their computers to work on your papers; you can't use them for just anything like in a regular lab, it has to just be your papers.

The use of the coordinating conjunction *but* causes a grammatical error. Remember, you use commas with coordinating conjunctions to connect two independent sentences.

14.5.2 Items in a List

Use a semicolon to separate items in a list that already contain commas themselves. This provides clarity for your reader

The hours are: Mon., Tues, Wed, Thu. 10 a.m.-6 p.m.; Fri. 10 a.m.-2 p.m.; and Sun.1-5 p.m.

14.6 The Colon (:)

14.6.1 To Illustrate

Use a colon after a complete sentence to directly relate the material following the colon to the previous sentence.

> Most professors, however, still hold to the black and white perspective: there is no "little bit" or "kinda" when it comes to academic honesty.

The colon indicates that the writer will explain what the black and white perspective is.

Do not use a colon after the following terms: *includes, including, to be* verbs, *such as*

Faulty sentence:

> The hours are: Mon., Tues., Wed., Thu. 10 a.m.-6 p.m.; Fri. 10 a.m.-2 p.m.; and Sun.1-5 p.m.

Correct sentence:

> The hours are Mon., Tues., Wed., Thu. 10 a.m.-6 p.m.; Fri. 10 a.m.-2 p.m.; and Sun.1-5 p.m.

14.6.2 In Salutations

Use a colon in the salutation of a business letter.

> Dear Mr. Smith:

14.6.3 In a Title

Use a colon to separate a main title from a subtitle.

> *Bob Costas: A True Broadcasting Everyman*

14.7 The Apostrophe (')

14.7.1 Possession

1.   Use an apostrophe to show possession in a singular noun.

Faulty sentence:

> Academic dishonesty begins quite early in a students academic

career.

Corrected sentence:

Academic dishonesty begins quite early in a student's academic career.

Students without an apostrophe indicates multiple students. *Student's* with the apostrophe indicates possession.

2. Use an apostrophe to show possession in a plural noun.

But maybe we can agree at least that we can try to broaden students' perspectives and raise their standards, so that they can be better critics -- and better self-critics.

Because the perspectives belong to multiple students, the apostrophe goes after the s.

3. Use an -'s at the end of the second item when indicating joint ownership.

Mary and Suzy's bistro

This example indicates that the bistro is jointly owned by Mary and Suzy.

4. Use an -'s at the end of each item when showing two or more separate owners.

Tom's and Frank's bistros

This example indicates that Tom and Frank each *individually* own a bistro.

5. Do not use an apostrophe when using possessive pronouns.

Faulty sentence:

Academic honesty and it's cousin plagiarism are two terms that students should become familiar with in their college career.

Correct sentence:

Academic honesty and its cousin plagiarism are two terms that students should become familiar with in their college career.

14.7.2 Omission

Use an apostrophe to show omission of letters, as in contractions; however, many instructors frown on the use of contractions in formal, academic writing.

> After looking at the IPFW statement on academic honesty it's clear that cheating is considered academic dishonesty, but what else falls under that umbrella?

Use an apostrophe to show omission of letters, as in abbreviations.

> 'Twas the night before Christmas

The apostrophe in this situation replaces the *I* of "It was."

14.7.3 Other Uses

Use -'s to make lowercase letters, abbreviations with periods, and example words plural.

> She finds there are too many b's in the nursery rhyme.

Do not use an apostrophe to make numbers or capital letters plural.

> She hopes that she earns As on all her tests.

14.8 Quotation Marks (" ")

14.8.1 Quoted Material

Use quotation marks to indicate quoted material. Quotation marks must **always** work in pairs. If you have open quotation marks, you **must** have closing quotation marks. Also, quotations within quotations use single quotation marks.

Faulty quotation:

> **BEGINNING AND ENDING QUOTES WITH ELLIPSES**
> Generally, it's unnecessary to begin or end a quote with ellipses. It is assumed by your reader that there is material both before and after your quote.

Thompson writes, "The college freshman sitting across from me in my office looked me in the eye and insisted vehemently that he didn't know why his paper was a word-for-word rendition of its twin, which I had found on the Web and was holding next to his own. Another student, having waited 3 days until I returned his graded essay—a cut-and-paste collage of several Web sources labeled "final"—assured me that he had simply given me an incorrect draft. A third brought his mother to the conference; it turned out that not only had she prepared the paper for him, but she also had done the plagiarizing (2439).

Correct quotations:

Thompson writes, "The college freshman sitting across from me in my office looked me in the eye and insisted vehemently that he didn't know why his paper was a word-for-word rendition of its twin, which I had found on the Web and was holding next to his own. Another student, having waited 3 days until I returned his graded essay—a cut-and-paste collage of several Web sources labeled 'final'—assured me that he had simply given me an incorrect draft. A third brought his mother to the conference; it turned out that not only had she prepared the paper for him, but she also had done the plagiarizing" (2439).

14.8.2 Irony

Use quotation marks to indicate irony sparingly, as it's commonly considered informal use. Quotation marks to emphasize information is generally frowned upon; instead try bold or italics.

Faulty sentence:

Most professors, however, still hold to the black and white perspective: there is no "little bit" or "kinda" when it comes to academic honesty.

Corrected sentence:

Most professors, however, still hold to the black and white perspective: there is no *little bit* or *kinda* when it comes to academic honesty.

14.8.3 Terminology

Use quote marks when referring to a term. Some texts also indicate single quotes are more acceptable for this function.

14.8.4 Titles

Use quote marks for titles of the smaller parts of whole items: article titles, songs, television episodes, book chapters, etc.

THE PART OF A WHOLE RULE

When deciding if something should be in quotes or underlined or italicized in MLA, consider the Part of a Whole Rule. Parts of things are in quotes; whole things are underlined or italicized. For example, an article in a magazine is in quotes; the magazine itself would be underlined or italicized. An album would be underlined or italicized, but a song on the album would be in quotes.

Faulty Sentence:

> However, in *Immunisation: Are Parents Making Informed Decisions?* Marfe contends...

Corrected sentence:

> However, in "Immunisation: Are Parents Making Informed Decisions?" Marfe contends...

14.9 The Hyphen (-) and Dash (–, —)

14.9.1 Hyphens

The hyphen is visually shorter than the dash (normally located to the right of the 0 key on the top row of a keyboard). Use a hyphen when expressing a compound modifier.

> I suppose we could just view anti-plagiarism instruction as a necessary evil, not particularly educational in the positive sense, but necessary.

> **WORD PROCESSING THE HYPHEN**
> Do not manually hyphenate your document. Let WordWrat do its job.

When listing hyphenated material, suspend the hyphen:

> The benefits are available for full- and part-time employees.

14.9.2 The En Dash (–)

The en dash is visually longer than the hyphen and shorter than the em dash.

- Use the en dash to replace the hyphen in compound terms when one element of the compound term is itself a hyphenated two- or three-word element.

> The hours are Mon., Tues, Wed, Thu. 10 a.m.–6 p.m.; Fri. 10 a.m.–2 p.m.; and Sun.1–5 p.m.

- Use the en dash in place of the word *through*.

> The hours are: Mon.–Thu. 10 a.m.–6 p.m.; Fri. 10 a.m.–2 p.m.; and Sun.1–5 p.m.

14.9.3 The Em Dash (—)

The em dash is what you know as the dash. Microsoft Word will create an em dash when you type two hyphens.

Use an em dash to emphasize information.

> What's most astounding, though—and most insulting — is that students plagiarize in ways that are so easy to catch.

14.10 Parentheses (())

Parenthetical marks are always used in pairs; if you open parentheses, be sure to close them.

- Use parenthesis to de-emphasize information.

> The instructions (see page 10 of your booklet) will detail how to select the proper insurance program for your family.

- Use parenthesis to indicate in-text citation.

> Many students who cheat blame faculty for their transgressions, especially professors who fail to respond to what students consider obvious incidents of cheating that occur in their courses (McCabe and Trevino, 2002).

14.11 Brackets ([])

Like parentheses, brackets are used in pairs. Never open a bracket without closing it.

- Use brackets to clarify information within a quote.

- Use brackets for information within parentheses.

WHAT'S [SIC]?
The bracketed term [sic] within a quote means "thus in the original." It's used to clarify for your reader that the error within a quote is the original author's, not your typo.

14.12 Ellipses (...)

Use ellipses to indicate material has been removed from a quote. Remember that even though you're removing material, you should still maintain the author's original intent.

> Some students complain that their professors are cheating them by spending more time consulting and publishing than teaching or preparing for classes. ...Notwithstanding outside influences, cheating is strongly dependent on what occurs in the classroom and the biggest factor is the instructor.

14.13 The Slash [/]

The slash is considered standard usage in composition; however, the backslash is not—it's best to never use the backslash.

Use the slash to connect words of equal value (*and/or*, *he/she*). There should be no spaces before or after the slash.

15. Mechanics

15.1 Capitalization

15.1.1 The First Word in a Sentence

The first word of a sentence is always capitalized.

Example:

> Academic honesty and its cousin plagiarism are two terms that students should become familiar with in their college career.

15.1.2 Proper Nouns and Adjectives

Proper nouns and proper adjectives are always capitalized.

Example:

> The Writing Center is conveniently located.

Capitalization is not necessary if the writer is not referring to a specific writing center.

15.1.3 Titles of Documents

Titles of printed works are capitalized except for conjunctions, articles, and prepositions of four or fewer letters.

Example:

> However, in "Immunisation: Are Parents Making Informed Decisions?" Marfe contends...

15.1.4 Professional Titles

Capitalize professional titles if they precede a person's name.

Examples:

> Instructor Smith, Reverend Thomas, Professor Martin

15.1.5 Poetry

Captialize the first letter of a line of poetry.

Example:

> There is a place where the sidewalk ends/ And before the street begins,/ And there the grass grows soft and white,/And there the sun burns crimson bright,/And there the moon-bird rests from his flight/ To cool in the peppermint wind.

15.1.6 Specific Names or Titles

Capitalize the specific name of a course, flight, gate, etc.; however, do not capitalize the general description.

Example:

> My English W129 instructor said in class though that it's better to go in person than online.

15.2 Number Use

15.2.1 Numbers Expressed as Words

15.2.1.1 Ten and Under

Generally, the numbers ten and under are expressed as words.

Example:

> Academic honesty and its cousin plagiarism are two terms that students should become familiar with in their college career.

15.2.1.2 Beginning a Sentence

When a number begins a sentence, it is expressed as a word.

Example:

> Fifty-four of the documented cases were imported from other countries, and 63 of the 64 measles patients had never been vaccinated against the disease.

15.2.2 Numbers Expressed as Numerals

15.2.2.1 Numbers Over Ten

Generally, numbers over ten are expressed as numerals.

Example:

> Federal health officials who track measles cases declared the United States virtually free of the disease in 2000, with yearly reported cases between 2000 and 2007 ranging from 29 to 116.

If a sentence contains numbers that can be expressed as either numerals or words, select one and be consistent.

15.2.2.2 Specific Situations

When using technical terms, dates, addresses, and measurements, numbers should be expressed as numerals.

Example:

> The research findings showed that 40 percent of almost 50,000 undergraduates questioned have plagiarized from the Net, up from only 10 percent in 1999.

15.3 Spelling

A quick Google search of "commonly misspelled words" will result in many such lists. It behooves you to become familiar with the words you frequently misspell.

Often misspelling is the result of using an incorrect word. For example, their/there, weather/whether, and its/it's. Spell-check will not catch this type of spelling mistake. When in doubt, check the dictionary.

COMPUTER TIP
DESCRIPTION

You can use Microsoft Word's Find and Replace feature to quickly select and correct any words you may have misspelled multiple times in your document.

Notes

Appendix A Databases and Indexes

The following is a comprehensive list compiled by Helmke Library indicating what databases and indexes are appropriate for each area of study. The titles under General and Multidisciplinary (see section 5.2.3) have been removed from each topic. It is recommended that you begin your search in the General and Multidisciplinary databases and indexes and then move to the more specialized databases and indexes.

To find any of the databases and indexes listed, visit **Find Resources By...** on the main page of Helmke's website, and then select **Subject A-Z**.

Accounting

- ABI/INFORM Suite
- Accounting & Tax Index
- ACM Digital Library
- Business Periodicals Index
- Business Source Premier
- Fed in Print
- Mergent Online
- Value Line Investment Survey

African American Studies

- International Index to Black Periodicals

American History

- America: History and Life
- American Periodical Series Online, 17401900
- Black Thought and Culture
- Historical New York Times
- In the First Person
- International Index to Black Periodicals
- Readers' Guide to Periodical Literature

American Studies

- America: History and Life
- American Film Scripts Online
- American Periodical Series Online, 17401900
- Black Thought and Culture

- Fort Wayne.com
- Historical New York Times
- Informe!
- International Index to Black Periodicals
- Lit Finder
- McClatchyTribune Collection
- National Newspapers
- Newslink
- Newspaper Source
- Poole's Index to Periodical Literature
- Television News Archive
- Women's Studies International
- Worldwide Political Science Abstracts
- Wright American Fiction 1851-1875

Anthropology
- Anthropology Plus
- Art Index
- Handbook of Latin American Studies
- Popline
- Women's Studies International

Architectural Engineering Technology
- Architectural Index
- Art Index
- ASCE American Society of Civil Engineers Journals
- Compendex

Arts & Humanities
- America: History and Life
- American Film Institute Catalog
- American Film Scripts Online
- Annual Bibliography of English Language and Literature (ABELL)
- Anthropology Plus
- Asian American Drama
- Black Drama 1850 to Present
- Book Review Digest

- Digital Images Delivered Online (DIDO)
- Dissertations and Theses
- Essay and General Literature Index
- Film Index International
- Handbook of Latin American Studies
- In the First Person
- IngentaConnect
- International Index
- International Index to Musical Periodicals
- International Index to Performing Arts Full Text
- Lit Finder
- Literature Criticism Online
- MLA International Bibliography
- North American Women's Drama
- OneSearch
- Periodicals Archive Online
- Periodicals Index Online
- Professional Development Collection
- Project MUSE
- Social Sciences and Humanities Index

Audiology & Speech Sciences
- Biomedical Reference Collections
- Cochrane Central Register of Controlled Trials (CCTR)
- Cochrane Database of Systematic Reviews
- Communication & Mass Media Complete
- Health and Psychosocial Instruments
- Medline (Ovid)
- Your Journals@Ovid

Biography
- Biography and Genealogy Master Index
- Biography Index
- Biography Resource Center
- Black Thought and Culture
- Historical New York Times

- Indiana Biography Index
- Television News Archive
- Women's Studies International

Biology

- Biological Sciences
- Biology Digest
- BioOne
- BIOSIS Previews
- Conference Papers Index
- EBSCO Animals
- EMBASE
- GreenFILE
- Herplit Database
- INSPIRE Image Collection
- Medline (EBSCO)
- Medline (ProQuestCSA)
- National Reference Center for Bioethics Literature
- Plant Science (CSA)

Books

- Amazon.com
- Book Review Digest
- Book Review Index
- Choice Reviews
- Library, Information Science & Technology Abstracts
- Professional Development Collection

Business

- ABI/INFORM Suite
- Business Source Premier
- Corporate ResourceNet
- CQ Researcher
- IngentaConnect
- LexisNexis Academic
- LexisNexis Corporate Affiliations
- MarketLine Business Information Center

- Mergent Online
- Regional Business News
- SourceOECD
- STATUSA / Internet
- Value Line Investment Survey

Careers & Employment

- ABI/INFORM Suite
- Mental Measurements Yearbook Indexes
- Mergent Online

Chemistry

- American Chemical Society Journals & Magazines
- Medline (EBSCO)
- Medline (ProQuestCSA)
- SciFinder Scholar
- STN Easy (Chemical Abstracts)
- STN on the Web (Chemical Abstracts)
- ToxLine (CSA)
- ToxLine (U.S. National Library of Medicine)
- ToxNet (U.S. National Library of Medicine)

Children's Literature

- Literature Criticism Online
- Short Story Index

Civil Engineering & Civil Engineering Technology

- Art Index
- ASCE American Society of Civil Engineers Journals
- Compendex

Communication

- Bibliography for Rhetoric, Composition, and Professional Communication
- Communication & Mass Media Complete
- INSPIRE Image Collection
- WorldNewspapers.com

Computer Engineering & Computer Engineering Technology

- ACM Digital Library

- Compendex
- Conference Papers Index
- IEEE AllSociety Periodicals Package

Computer Science

- ABI/INFORM Suite
- ACM Digital Library
- Compendex
- IEEE AllSociety Periodicals Package

Construction Engineering Technology

- Art Index
- Compendex

Consumer & Family Sciences

- Biomedical Reference Collections
- CINAHL (EBSCO)
- Health and Psychosocial Instruments
- Health Source: Consumer Edition
- Medline (Ovid)
- PreCINAHL (EBSCO)
- Your Journals@Ovid

Consumer Health

- CINAHL (EBSCO)
- PreCINAHL (EBSCO)

Counseling

- Criminal Justice Periodicals Index
- Education Full Text
- Education Index
- ERIC
- ERIC (CSA)
- Teacher Reference Center

Courts

- Criminal Justice Periodicals Index
- Index to Legal Periodicals and Books
- LexisNexis Academic

Criminal Justice

- ABI/INFORM Suite
- Criminal Justice Abstracts
- Criminal Justice Periodicals Index
- Criminology: a SAGE FullText Collection
- Urban Affairs Abstracts

Dental Education

- ACPJournal Club
- Biomedical Reference Collections
- CINAHL (EBSCO)
- Cochrane Central Register of Controlled Trials (CCTR)
- Cochrane Database of Systematic Reviews
- EMBASE
- Health and Psychosocial Instruments
- Health Source: Consumer Edition
- Healthstar
- Journals@Ovid (Full Text)
- Lancet Archive
- Medline (EBSCO)
- Medline (Ovid)
- PreCINAHL (EBSCO)
- Your Journals@Ovid

Early Childhood Education

- Education Full Text
- Education Index
- ERIC
- ERIC (CSA)
- Teacher Reference Center

Economics

- ABC/Pol Sci
- ABI/INFORM Suite
- Accounting & Tax Index
- ACM Digital Library
- Anthropology Plus
- Business Source Premier

- EconLit
- Fed in Print
- SourceOECD

Education

- Book Review Digest
- Dissertations and Theses
- Education Full Text
- Education Index
- ERIC
- ERIC (CSA)
- IngentaConnect
- International Index to Musical Periodicals
- Mental Measurements Yearbook Indexes
- OneSearch
- Primary Search
- Professional Development Collection
- Teacher Reference Center

Electrical Engineering & Electrical Engineering Technology

- ACM Digital Library
- Compendex
- Conference Papers Index
- IEEE AllSociety Periodicals Package

Elementary Education

- Education Full Text
- Education Index
- ERIC
- ERIC (CSA)
- Teacher Reference Center

Engineering, Technology, & Computer Science

- ACM Digital Library
- ASCE American Society of Civil Engineers Journals
- Compendex
- Conference Papers Index
- Dissertations and Theses

- IEEE AllSociety Periodicals Package
- IngentaConnect
- SciFinder Scholar
- STN Easy (Chemical Abstracts)
- STN on the Web (Chemical Abstracts)

English

- American Film Institute Catalog
- Annual Bibliography of English Language and Literature (ABELL)
- Film Index International
- Humanities Index
- International Index to Performing Arts Full Text
- Lit Finder
- Literature Criticism Online
- MLA International Bibliography
- Short Story Index
- Wright American Fiction 1851-1875

Finance

- ABI/INFORM Suite
- Accounting & Tax Index
- Business Periodicals Index
- Business Source Premier
- EconLit
- Fed in Print
- Mergent Online
- Value Line Investment Survey

Fine Arts

- Art Index
- Digital Images Delivered Online (DIDO)
- Humanities Index

Folklore

- America: History and Life
- Annual Bibliography of English Language and Literature (ABELL)
- Anthropology Plus
- Humanities Index

- MLA International Bibliography
- Women's Studies International

French

- Annual Bibliography of English Language and Literature (ABELL)
- Humanities Index
- MLA International Bibliography

Geosciences

- GeoRef
- GeoScienceWorld
- ToxLine (CSA)
- ToxLine (U.S. National Library of Medicine)
- ToxNet (U.S. National Library of Medicine)

German

- Annual Bibliography of English Language and Literature (ABELL)
- Humanities Index
- MLA International Bibliography

Gerontology

- AARP Ageline
- Medline (Ovid)
- PubMed

Government

- Congressional Record Index
- CQ Researcher
- History of Bills
- Index to Current Urban Documents
- Index to Legal Periodicals and Books
- Indianapolis Star
- IngentaConnect
- Military and Government Collection
- PAIS (Public Affairs Information Service) Bulletin

Health Sciences & Medicine

- AARP Ageline
- ACPJournal Club
- Alcohol and Alcohol Problems Science Database

- Anthropology Plus
- Bioethics Research from the Kennedy Institute of Ethics
- Biomedical Reference Collections
- Cancer.gov (PubMed)
- CINAHL (EBSCO)
- Cochrane Central Register of Controlled Trials (CCTR)
- Cochrane Database of Systematic Reviews
- Database of Abstracts of Reviews of Effects
- Dissertations and Theses
- EBM Reviews Full Text
- EMBASE
- Health Business FullTEXT
- Health Source: Consumer Edition
- Health Source: Nursing/Academic Edition
- Health Technology Assessment
- Healthstar
- IngentaConnect
- Journals@Ovid (Full Text)
- Lancet Archive
- Medline (EBSCO)
- Medline (NLM Gateway)
- Medline (Ovid)
- Medline (ProQuestCSA)
- MEDLINE® Daily Update
- MEDLINE® InProcess & Other NonIndexed Citations (PREM)
- National Reference Center for Bioethics Literature
- NHS Economic Evaluation Database
- OLDMEDLINE
- OneSearch
- Popline
- PreCINAHL (EBSCO)
- PubMed
- TRIP (Turning Research Into Practice) Database
- Your Journals@Ovid

Health Services

- Biomedical Reference Collections
- CINAHL (EBSCO)
- Health and Psychosocial Instruments
- Health Business FullTEXT
- Health Source: Consumer Edition
- Health Technology Assessment
- Healthstar
- Medline (Ovid)
- NHS Economic Evaluation Database
- Popline
- PreCINAHL (EBSCO)
- Your Journals@Ovid

History

- ABC/Pol Sci
- America: History and Life
- Anthropology Plus
- Black Thought and Culture
- Handbook of Latin American Studies
- Historical New York Times
- In the First Person
- Indianapolis Newspapers Database, 1979-1991
- Indianapolis Star
- INSPIRE Image Collection
- International Index to Black Periodicals
- New York Times Index
- PAIS Bulletin
- Periodicals Archive Online
- Periodicals Index Online
- Poole's Index to Periodical Literature
- Readers' Guide to Periodical Literature
- Women's Studies International
- Worldwide Political Science Abstracts
- Wright American Fiction 1851-1875

Hospitality & Tourism Management

- ABI/INFORM Suite
- Business Source Premier
- Regional Business News
- Value Line Investment Survey

Industrial Engineering Technology

- Compendex
- Conference Papers Index

Informatics, Information Systems, & Information Technology

- ABI/INFORM Suite
- ACM Digital Library
- Compendex
- IEEE AllSociety Periodicals Package

Interior Design

- Art Index
- Compendex
- Humanities Index
- PsycINFO
- Sociological Abstracts

Journalism

- American Periodical Series Online, 1740-1900
- Communication & Mass Media Complete
- Editorials on File
- FortWayne.com
- Indianapolis Star
- INSPIRE Image Collection
- LexisNexis Corporate Affiliations
- New York Times Index

Labor Studies

- ABI/INFORM Suite
- America: History and Life
- PAIS Bulletin
- SourceOECD
- Worldwide Political Science Abstracts

Latin American History

- Handbook of Latin American Studies

Laws

- Congressional Record Index
- Criminal Justice Periodicals Index
- History of Bills

Linguistics

- Anthropology Plus
- Humanities Index

Management & Administration

- ABI/INFORM Suite
- Business Periodicals Index
- Business Source Premier
- Corporate ResourceNet
- EconLit
- Fed in Print
- Health Business FullTEXT
- Knowledge@Wharton
- MarketLine Business Information Center
- Mergent Online
- Value Line Investment Survey

Maps

- INSPIRE Image Collection

Marketing

- ABI/INFORM Suite
- Business Periodicals Index
- Business Source Premier
- Corporate ResourceNet
- EconLit
- Knowledge@Wharton
- SourceOECD

Mathematics

- (see also Science and Mathematics)
- MathSciNet

Mechanical Engineering & Mechanical Engineering Technology

- ACM Digital Library
- Compendex
- Conference Papers Index

Media & Public Communication

- American Film Institute Catalog
- Bibliography for Rhetoric, Composition, and Professional Communication
- Communication & Mass Media Complete
- Editorials on File
- Indianapolis Star
- INSPIRE Image Collection
- Newslink
- Onlinenewspapers.com
- WorldNewspapers.com

Music

- Humanities Index
- International Index to Musical Periodicals
- International Index to Performing Arts Full Text

Native American Studies

- ABI/INFORM Suite
- Alternative Press Index
- America: History and Life
- Anthropology Plus
- Art Index
- Handbook of Latin American Studies

News & Current Events

- ABI/INFORM Suite
- Corporate ResourceNet
- CQ Researcher
- Editorials on File
- FortWayne.com
- Historical New York Times
- Indianapolis Newspapers Database, 1979-1991

- Indianapolis Star
- Informe!
- INSPIRE Image Collection
- LexisNexis Academic
- MasterFILE Premier
- McClatchy Tribune Collection
- Mergent Online
- National Newspapers
- New York Times Index
- Newslink
- Newspaper Source
- Onlinenewspapers.com
- Regional Business News
- Television News Archive
- TOPICsearch
- WorldNewspapers.com

Nursing

- AARP Ageline
- ACPJournal Club
- Biomedical Reference Collections
- CINAHL (EBSCO)
- Cochrane Central Register of Controlled Trials (CCTR)
- Cochrane Database of Systematic Reviews
- EBM Reviews Full Text
- EMBASE
- Health and Psychosocial Instruments
- Health Source: Consumer Edition
- Health Source: Nursing/Academic Edition
- Health Technology Assessment
- Healthstar
- Journals@Ovid (Full Text)
- Lancet Archive
- Medline (EBSCO)
- Medline (Ovid)
- National Reference Center for Bioethics Literature

- Popline
- PreCINAHL (EBSCO)
- TRIP (Turning Research Into Practice) Database
- Your Journals@Ovid

Organizational Leadership & Supervision

- ABC/Pol Sci
- ABI/INFORM Suite

Peace & Conflict Studies

- ABC/Pol Sci
- Alternative Press Index
- Military and Government Collection
- Philosopher's Index
- SourceOECD
- Worldwide Political Science Abstracts

Philosophy

- Humanities Index
- National Reference Center for Bioethics Literature
- Philosopher's Index

Physics

- Conference Papers Index
- MathSciNet
- Physical Review Online Archive (PROLA)
- Physics Web

Political Science

- ABC/Pol Sci
- America: History and Life
- EconLit
- Indianapolis Star
- International Political Science Abstracts
- PAIS (Public Affairs Information Service) Bulletin
- Worldwide Political Science Abstracts

Popular Culture

- American Periodical Series Online, 17401900

Psychology

- Alcohol and Alcohol Problems Science Database
- Anthropology Plus
- Criminal Justice Abstracts
- Criminology: a SAGE FullText Collection
- Mental Measurements Yearbook Indexes
- PsycARTICLES
- PsycINFO
- Social Services Abstracts

Public & Environmental Affairs

- ABC/Pol Sci
- ABI/INFORM Suite
- Criminal Justice Periodicals Index
- EconLit
- Fed in Print
- GreenFILE
- Health Business FullTEXT
- Index to Current Urban Documents
- Indianapolis Newspapers Database, 19791991
- Indianapolis Star
- PAIS (Public Affairs Information Service) Bulletin
- SourceOECD
- Urban Affairs Abstracts
- Worldwide Political Science Abstracts

Regulations

- Fed in Print

Religious Studies

- Anthropology Plus
- Humanities Index
- Philosopher's Index

School Administration

- Education Full Text
- Education Index
- ERIC

- ERIC (CSA)
- Teacher Reference Center

Sciences & Mathematics
- Agricola (Agricultural Online Access)
- Biological & Agricultural Index
- Biological Sciences
- Biology Digest
- BioOne
- Cancer.gov (PubMed)
- Conference Papers Index
- Dissertations and Theses
- EBSCO Animals
- General Science Index
- GeoRef
- GeoScienceWorld
- IngentaConnect
- Lancet Archive
- MathSciNet
- Medline (EBSCO)
- Medline (NLM Gateway)
- Medline (Ovid)
- Medline (ProQuestCSA)
- MEDLINE® Daily Update
- MEDLINE® InProcess & Other NonIndexed Citations (PREM)
- National Reference Center for Bioethics Literature
- OLDMEDLINE
- OneSearch
- PubMed
- Science.gov
- SciFinder Scholar
- ToxLine (U.S. National Library of Medicine)
- ToxNet (U.S. National Library of Medicine)

Secondary Education
- Education Full Text

- Education Index
- ERIC
- ERIC (CSA)
- MAS Ultra: School Edition
- Teacher Reference Center

Serials (Journals, Magazines, Periodicals)

- Dialog Journal Name Finder
- Editorials on File

Social Sciences

- Alternative Press Index
- America: History and Life
- Anthropology Plus
- Black Thought and Culture
- Book Review Digest
- Communication & Mass Media Complete
- Criminal Justice Abstracts
- Criminology: a SAGE FullText Collection
- Dissertations and Theses
- Essay and General Literature Index
- GreenFILE
- Handbook of Latin American Studies
- Health and Psychosocial Instruments
- In the First Person
- IngentaConnect
- International Index
- Mental Measurements Yearbook Indexes
- National Reference Center for Bioethics Literature
- OneSearch
- PAIS (Public Affairs Information Service) Bulletin
- Periodicals Archive Online
- Periodicals Index Online
- Popline
- Project MUSE
- PsycARTICLES

- PsycINFO
- Social Sciences and Humanities Index
- Social Sciences Index
- Social Services Abstracts
- Sociological Abstracts
- Women's Studies International
- Worldwide Political Science Abstracts

Sociology

- Alcohol and Alcohol Problems Science Database
- Alternative Press Index
- Anthropology Plus
- Black Thought and Culture
- Criminal Justice Abstracts
- Criminal Justice Periodicals Index
- Criminology: a SAGE FullText Collection
- Mental Measurements Yearbook Indexes
- PAIS Bulletin
- Social Services Abstracts
- Sociological Abstracts
- Women's Studies International

Software Engineering

- ABI/INFORM Suite
- ACM Digital Library
- Compendex
- IEEE AllSociety Periodicals Package

Spanish

- Annual Bibliography of English Language and Literature
- Humanities Index
- Informe!
- MLA International Bibliography

Statistics & Facts

- ABI/INFORM Suite
- CQ Researcher
- Fed in Print

- LexisNexis Corporate Affiliations
- MarketLine Business Information Center
- SourceOECD
- STATUSA / Internet

Systems Engineering

- ACM Digital Library
- Compendex
- IEEE AllSociety Periodicals Package

Theatre

- American Film Scripts Online
- Asian American Drama
- Black Drama 1850 to Present
- Humanities Index
- International Index to Performing Arts Full Text
- Lit Finder
- MLA International Bibliography
- New York Times Index
- North American Women's Drama

Visual Communication & Design

- ACM Digital Library
- Art Index
- Digital Images Delivered Online (DIDO)
- Humanities Index
- INSPIRE Image Collection

Women's Studies

- Alternative Press Index
- America: History and Life
- American Periodical Series Online, 1740-1900
- Black Thought and Culture
- North American Women's Drama
- Women's Studies International
- Wright American Fiction 1851-1875

Writing (Creative, Professional, Technical)

- Bibliography for Rhetoric, Composition, and Professional

Communication

- Humanities Index
- MLA International Bibliography
- Short Story Index